Also by Melanie Phillips

*The Builder's Stone: How Jews and Christians Built
the West—and Why Only They Can Save It*

FIGHTING

THE

HATE

FIGHTING THE HATE

A Handbook for Jews Under Siege

MELANIE PHILLIPS

WICKED SON

A WICKED SON BOOK
An Imprint of Post Hill Press
ISBN: 979-8-89565-630-3
ISBN (eBook): 979-8-89565-631-0

Fighting the Hate:
A Handbook for Jews Under Siege
© 2026 by Melanie Phillips
All Rights Reserved

Cover Design by Jim Villaflores

Post Hill Press
New York • Nashville
wickedsonbooks.com
posthillpress.com

Published in the United States of America
1 2 3 4 5 6 7 8 9 10

To all who are defending the Jewish people:

חזק חזק ונתחזק

Be strong, be strong, and let us strengthen each other.

CONTENTS

CHAPTER 1

WHAT HAS HAPPENED

• • • •

How should the Jewish world fight back against the lunacy that has engulfed the West since the Hamas-led atrocities in Israel on October 7, 2023? How do you cope when a civilization is collapsing around your ears?

Diaspora Jews are currently reeling from a crisis of legitimacy and acceptance that is unprecedented in nature and scale even by the standards of their uniquely beleaguered history.

Persecuted and murdered in one country after another throughout the past two millennia, they have never before faced simultaneous attacks across continents as they do today.

The starting gun for this campaign of demonization and attacks against Israel and diaspora Jews was fired by the biggest and most barbaric single attack on the Jewish people since the Holocaust—the slaughter of some 1,200 women, children, and men in southern Israel and the kidnapping of more than 250 hostages on October 7, 2023.

During the war that followed, Islamist groups and the far left conducted a concerted and spectacularly successful attempt to manipulate Western public opinion—through an unstoppable and overwhelming torrent of lies and distortions—into delegitimizing Israel, all as a means to its eventual destruction.

Jews in Britain, America, Canada, Australia, and elsewhere have been physically attacked, accused of being baby killers, abused in restaurants, excluded from sporting and cultural events, and socially and professionally ostracized. New blood libels alleging monstrous Israeli behavior have been manufactured almost every day. Allegations have multiplied, stating that Israel is responsible for starvation and famine in Gaza, is intent upon committing genocide, and is wantonly killing Gazan civilians. Despite clear evidence that these were wild falsehoods, they were widely believed and achieved the status of settled fact.

In America, support for Israel has been dropping like a stone as Jews are defamed and attacked. Jewish students on campuses on both sides of the Atlantic face widespread intimidation and abuse. The Palestinian flag, regarded by many Jews as akin to the Nazi swastika because it is the emblem of a movement that seeks to erase Jewish national identity and history, has become a branded logo displayed on walls, streetlights, clothing, and other artifacts. In Britain, Jewish patients seeking medical treatment are increasingly nervous about using the National Health Service because so many medical and nursing staff have been wearing this symbol on their uniforms.

Far from dampening down this incendiary atmosphere, political leaders in Britain, Europe, and Australia have fanned the flames still further by repeating the false accusations of unconscionable Israeli behavior, even while all available evidence suggested the very opposite was the case.

In America, where the political situation since the arrival of Donald Trump in the White House has been very different, Jews are also feeling increasingly unsafe. An article from the American Jewish Committee about the organization's *2024 Survey of American Jewish Opinion* recorded the effects of the October 7 attack. It noted:

> More than half…said they have avoided talking about the Israel-Hamas war with other people and [almost half] said they felt unsafe sharing their views on Israel on social media. More than one in ten…adults said they ended a friendship or relationship with a person since October 7 because they expressed antisemitic views. Twenty-seven percent…said they have hidden their Jewish identity or have chosen not to disclose it when meeting someone new since the war began. And between 7 and 14 percent said they have considered moving to another country due to antisemitism.[1]

The forces involved in this onslaught against Israel and the Jews are enormous—global, highly organized, and hugely funded. By definition, antisemitism, which is based on an irrational and paranoid hatred of Jews that's hardwired into Western culture, can't be tackled through facts and evidence. The number of Muslims in the West who are intent on conquering it for Islam and who are masterminding this onslaught is also increasing exponentially. So, a fatalistic attitude is growing that suggests it's all over for Western civilization and for the Jews of the diaspora.

After the publication in January 2025 of my book, *The Builder's Stone: How Jews and Christians Built the West—and Why Only They Can Save It,* I visited America, Australia, and Britain to promote it. In all three countries, I spoke at meeting after meeting with Jews who were near stupefied by the terrifying hatred and irrationality that was unfolding all around them.

The scale and nature of this bombardment was "gaslighting" them badly, making them doubt their own grip on reality when it seemed that the entire world of liberal opinion was unanimous in denouncing and demonizing Israel. "Were any of these claims true?" they wondered. How could they possibly all be *untrue* if everyone—not just the mainstream media but also respected international bodies like the United Nations and World Health Organization, international courts like the International Criminal Court and International Court of Justice, big humanitarian nongovernmental organizations like Amnesty International, Human Rights Watch, and Doctors Without Borders, and the governments of countries like Britain, France, Canada, and Australia—was saying the same thing? Was it really possible that they could all be wrong and Israel could be right?

At the same time, I encountered in all three countries Jews who don't think that what's happening is anything to get too worried about. For those Jews who usually live in Jewish areas, have mostly Jewish friends and work colleagues, or who feel so disconnected from Israel that the media campaign of defamation against the Jewish state—which is so all-encompassing in Britain—barely registers on their radar, it's still possible to live inside a bubble of relative tranquility. There are also many Jews who themselves support the progressive ideologies that are fueling the madness against Israel, and so, by definition, see nothing amiss except for the behavior of Israel, to whose clamorous denunciation they eagerly add their voices.

Even among those Jews who are rattled by the hatred that's erupted, some have also blamed Israel for making things bad for them. They assert that Israel's prime minister, Benjamin Netanyahu, has prolonged the war in Gaza, which has fueled so much hostility in the West, merely in order to stay in power. For similar reasons, they claim that he has followed the aggressive agenda of his "extremist" ministers, Bezalel Smotrich and Itamar Ben-Gvir, in order to prevent his coalition government from disintegrating.

Other diaspora Jews have dealt with their concern about the wave of hatred against them by saying it will all blow over, that this happens every time there's a war in Gaza, and that we've all been here before.

To which yet others have responded by noting that the same terrible cultural blindness was a hallmark of the Jews in Nazi Germany and signed their death warrant. They were engulfed by the Holocaust as a consequence of their delusion that their fellow Germans regarded them as no different from themselves. Many now fret that history may be repeating itself.

The differences between all these groups of Jews are stark. There is much bad blood between liberals who blame Netanyahu and conservatives who blame Hamas and Iran; between Jewish leaders paralyzed by fear and division and, opposing them, the communities they lead who accuse them of having abandoned the defense of the Jewish people; and between Jews who believe that they must make an alliance with any group fighting the Islamization of the West and those who fiercely draw the line against joining forces with far-right or neo-Nazi extremists.

Uppermost among the different Jewish communities in all three countries is a profound sense of disorientation and dislocation. Their acceptance as Americans, Australians, or Brits that so many had taken for granted has now blown up in their faces. Discovering that this acceptance was in fact an illusion all along, they have lost their bearings.

In Australia, this has come as a particularly savage blow, and the resulting distress and disorientation are therefore particularly severe. This is because, unlike other diaspora Jews, Australian Jews always felt very secure inside their national skin.

Australian society was overwhelmingly free of the kind of polite social contempt of Jews that was always present in Britain, let alone the antisemitic convulsions in France in the late nineteenth century that turned the secular Theodor Herzl into a Zionist and have intensified so badly across the West in recent years. Even in America, famously a melting pot for hyphenated Americans, Jews never lost the instinct to conform for their own protection to prevailing social trends arising from America's foundational Anglo-Saxon Protestant culture, as they also did to subsequent post-biblical secular ideologies of race and gender that became the dominant cultural narrative.

Having never had to cope with the permanent degree of at least low-level antisemitism of which British Jews in particular have always been uncomfortably aware, Australian Jews were not only left aghast but nonplussed by the outpouring of anti-Israel and anti-Jewish hysteria that erupted after the October 7 atrocities. When they observed demonstrators screaming murderous obscenities about the Jews at a rally outside the iconic Sydney Opera House two days after the attack on Israel, they went into a state of shock.

As Prime Minister Anthony Albanese's Labor government continuously added to the incitement by regurgitating defamatory falsehoods about Israel's supposed human rights abuses in Gaza, Australia's overwhelmingly Zionist Jews became increasingly horrified. For the first time, they felt isolated and threatened in their own country.

Far worse was to follow. Not only were synagogues firebombed, but in December 2025 fourteen Jews and a retired police officer were murdered and forty others wounded when two Islamist gunmen opened fire on a Chanukah candle-lighting ceremony on Sydney's Bondi beach.

When I visited Melbourne and Sydney earlier in the year, communal meetings were heavily guarded, and ticket holders were checked in advance against the names of known troublemakers. In Brisbane, when my hosts sought a larger hall for my speaking engagement, six venues, including the Queensland Cricketers' Club, turned them down on the basis that they refused to hold Jewish events—whether because of security fears or ideological conviction, it wasn't clear. "We never used to live like this," the Australian Jews told me, shaking their heads in disbelief. From enjoying the most relaxed and laid back of cultural lifestyles, they now felt as if they were living under siege.

In Britain, the Jewish community felt similarly betrayed by Sir Keir Starmer's Labour government, which recycled the same falsehoods and incitement. Many of London's Jews became too frightened to venture into central London on a Saturday because of the aggressive and intimidatory pro-Gaza demonstrations at which the police did next to nothing to prevent criminal chants threatening to destroy Israel, unleash a global "intifada," and murder Jews.

Back in the early aughties, British Jews had experienced an uncomfortable and all too prescient wake-up call about their deteriorating position. Israel's struggle to suppress the Second Intifada, in which more than 1,300 Israelis were murdered, provoked a level of Israel demonization and open antisemitism that led a number of British Jews to observe that they'd been living in a fool's paradise. In shocking contradiction of what they had so foolishly told themselves, they noted that antisemitism hadn't disappeared at all. It had merely taken a fifty-year break after the discovery of the Nazi extermination camps. Now, it was back.

Until the October 7, 2023, atrocities turned the world upside down, American Jews largely felt immune from these convulsions. These Jews perceived the increasing political power in Britain and Europe of Muslim communities—large numbers of whom were refusing to integrate and instead expecting Britain and Europe to become more Islamic—and wondered how long it would be before their British and European counterparts woke up to the peril they were in and left these countries that were becoming increasingly dangerous for them.

In fact, the overwhelming majority of those in Britain who were demonizing Israel at that time were the non-Muslim progressive left, along with some on the right. It didn't occur to most American Jews that similar forces were building in their own society and that they themselves might soon face a similar predicament. Viewing what was happening in Britain and Europe as nothing to do with them, they believed themselves to be in the safest and most benign environment for Jews on earth.

This feeling of immunity persisted even after the Council on American-Islamic Relations was indicted as a coconspirator in the 2008 Holy Land Foundation court case. At this trial, which revealed evidence of the links between the foundation and

Hamas, five of its leaders were convicted of terrorism, money laundering, and tax fraud. Even after the massacre in 2018 at the Tree of Life synagogue in Pittsburgh in which eleven worshippers were murdered by a white supremacist, most American Jews remained unperturbed by the implications for their own safety and that of America.

Nor were most American Jews particularly attached to or interested in Israel. Religious observance among them was a minority pursuit. The majority of them instead identified with and were preoccupied by progressive ideological causes such as abortion and the identity politics issues of race, sexuality, and gender. They were first and foremost Americans; their Jewish identity was an add-on, largely confined to signature and highly selective cultural markers such as using Yiddish words and phrases like "bubbele" (a term of endearment) or eating Jewish delicacies such as lox and bagels or blintzes.

Most British Jews similarly dismissed as alarmism any concerns about homegrown Muslim extremism. After the Second Intifada in Israel was finally suppressed in 2005, British Jews pushed to the back of their minds for the better part of two decades the unwelcome discovery they had made about their place in Britain. Their leaders campaigned against "Islamophobia" on the basis that this was the equivalent of antisemitism.

However well informed any of them might have been during those years, few in either Britain or America could have anticipated the monstrous reaction throughout the West to the October 7 atrocities in Israel. Few could have imagined the extent to which demonstrably false or ludicrous claims about Israel would become not just accepted but resistant to logic, evidence, or any kind of challenge based in reality. Few could have foreseen the nightmarish Jew hunts that took place in certain Western cities. Few could have believed how the police and the university authorities would stand aside from the incitement against Jews on the streets and on campuses, claiming the need to defend freedom of speech.

In America, few could have imagined the wave of attacks including the firebombing of Jews at a community event in Boulder, Colorado in June 2025 by a Muslim who wanted to kill "all Zionist people"; the gunning down, a few weeks earlier, of two Israel embassy staffers outside the Capital Jewish Museum in Washington DC by a man who posted online that he wanted to "vaporize every Israeli 18 and above"; or in November 2025, when a mob swarmed Manhattan's Park East synagogue chanting pro-intifada slogans and shouting at Jews arriving for a meeting inside that was providing information about emigration to Israel.

And in Britain, few foresaw the atrocity on Yom Kippur 2025, when a Muslim attacked a Manchester synagogue and left two worshippers dead—the first time that British Jews had been murdered at prayer since they were readmitted to Britain in the eighteenth century having been expelled in 1290.

It appeared to the flabbergasted and frightened Jews that their society had descended into a kind of lunacy that was embedded in the universities and—with precious few exceptions—not challenged by the media or any official authorities. Hardly anyone in public life called out the lies being told about Israel for what they were. On the contrary, political and cultural leaders themselves repeatedly echoed them.

Language was hijacked. "Zionist" became synonymous with "Nazi." "Genocide" was no longer understood to be the aim of Hamas, Hezbollah, and Iran, which had all sworn repeatedly to exterminate Israel and the Jews. Instead, Israel found itself grotesquely accused of genocide merely by going to war against its would-be exterminators. The most just and vital of wars was being reframed as a heinous crime against humanity.

Since Israel and Zionism were being framed as evil, it followed that its supporters would be framed as evil too. And since some 80 percent of Jews in Britain and America either identify as Zionists or say that caring about Israel is an essential or important part of what being Jewish means to them, this put a target on the back of every Jew.

Jews found to their horror that this lunacy was what now passed as unchallengeable fact among great swaths of the educated classes. In Britain, there was scarcely a profession or institution in which the majority did not believe that Israel was out of control in Gaza and wantonly killing or starving the innocent in great numbers.

The obsessional nature of all this, the sheer volume and frequency of these accusations, and the way they were being insinuated into almost every aspect of daily life that had no connection whatsoever with the Middle East, created a sense in the Jewish community of being under a sustained and nightmarish bombardment.

For many diaspora Jews, living under siege has become normalized. They hide identifying symbols such as Star of David necklaces or the uniform badges of their Jewish schools. Synagogues, Jewish communal organizations, and Jewish events have guards posted at the entrance. In Britain, some Jewish schools are behind barbed wire.

Many students on campus are forced to face institutionalized anti-Israel and anti-Jewish incitement. Some have decided as a result to avoid going to lectures. Others have decided the safest course of action is never to engage with anyone about Israel or "Palestine." Meanwhile, it's become standard procedure for

Jewish students to conceal the locations, dates, and times of their meetings, with some going to the elaborate lengths of publicizing fake venues to throw potential disruptors or worse off the scent.

Far from supporting and defending their Jewish communities, the governments of Britain, Australia, and Canada have been feeding the frenzy. Refusing to stop the intimidation of Jews by the pro-Gaza demonstrations, these governments added to the incitement by regurgitating wildly unfounded Hamas claims of Israeli war crimes of starving and deliberately killing Gazan civilians.

In all the places I visited, in London and New York, Boston and Los Angeles, Sydney and Melbourne, I found Jews in great distress and with a profound loss of bearings. They no longer recognized the country they were living in.

Everywhere I went, members of the Jewish community asked me the same urgent questions over and over again. What should we do? What *can* we do?

Disbelief sat alongside fear and confusion. People simply couldn't believe what they were seeing and hearing: the wild conspiracy theories about Jews; the total refusal to accept or even listen to any evidence about the Gaza war based on facts; the unhinged accusation that they themselves, in London, New York, or Melbourne, were somehow guilty of killing Palestinian babies.

They couldn't believe that people they'd known all their lives, friends and even family members, had turned against them purely because they stuck up for Israel or tried to present factual evidence to counter the lies.

"How should I respond to all this?" they asked over and over again. "Should I stand up for Israel in public? Even if that imperils my job, my livelihood, and my relationship with my family or my friends? Or should I protect myself by keeping out of any such trouble?"

Making all this far worse was that, even among those who supported Israel and were horrified by the lunacy, there was a nagging doubt about whether it really *was* lunacy or whether the accusations against Israel were true.

People would say to me that the antisemitism was terrible, they were horrified by all the lies and that so many were believing them, and the situation was dangerous and out of control—and then they'd say quietly, "But do you think there's any truth in any of it? Do you think Israel really *is* starving the Gazans?"

In other words, the power of the dreadfully distressing video images, in particular those being transmitted by broadcasting organizations along with the relentless and almost entirely unchallenged backdrop of claims of Israeli inhumanity and war crimes, was twisting the minds of even some Israel supporters.

In addition, people very reasonably asked another persistent set of questions: How can we believe anything that we read or watch about the war in Gaza? How can we judge which sources to trust? How can we find out what we need to know?

These are very important questions. People have never had so much information coming at them 24/7 about everything. Yet the more information there is, the less there is to be believed.

The Wild West of the internet is a force for both good and bad. On the one hand, it's enabled people who have realized that the mainstream media are lying to them to access alternative sources of information. On the other hand, the absence of editorial filters means that people have no easy or reliable way of working out what is untrue or distorted. So people have been ricocheting around the internet from one deeply misleading source to another.

Alongside their fear and bewilderment, not to mention their grief and despair over the October 7 victims, the plight of the hostages—the survivors of whom were finally released almost two years to the day after they were kidnapped into Gaza—and the steadily mounting losses of so many young Israelis fighting in the war, diaspora Jews have been experiencing great loneliness. The feeling of abandonment, of not having allies against a very great evil, and of finding that so many refuse to even acknowledge it as evil but have instead been turning on its victims, have all created a sense of isolation that has sometimes led into acute depression.

Among the diminishing number of Holocaust survivors and those who lived through the Second World War, there has been horror that the West appears to have learned nothing from the Nazi nightmare. Among younger British Jews, the shock delivered by this hostility from a modern western populace, whose benign and rational nature they had seen no reason to doubt, has been enormous.

Among Israelis, however, the response to the plight of diaspora Jews has been as simple as it is brutal. "Why are these Jews remaining in these countries?" ask the Israelis. "They should be here in Israel, fighting with us against our common enemies. This is their real homeland. Why can't they see it?"

To which the short answer is that it's often extremely difficult to accept that the game is up, not to mention the practical, emotional, and psychological difficulties of moving to another country—let alone a foreign and very different Middle East culture. Family ties also mean that moving to Israel isn't an option for many diaspora Jews.

Although more of them are now deciding to do so, the degree of threat to their safety would need to be significantly higher before this becomes a mass movement. In America, rising alarm among the Jewish community is more likely to merely accelerate their move out of states such as New York—where there's a liberal-Muslim axis that's perceived to be putting the Jews at increasing risk—into other states where this axis has no traction.

And some diaspora Jews are outraged by the idea that they should be, in effect, chased out of the country they call home and feel it is their duty to remain there and fight to continue as a diaspora Jew.

For the vast majority of such Jews who are staying put, the questions are urgent, and the dilemmas are desperate.

"Why is all this happening?" they ask. "When will it end? *Will* it ever end? Why are the police not protecting us but defending instead those who threaten us? Why aren't our leaders fighting back by rebutting all the lies and declaring the things that need to be said? Why isn't Israel doing a better job of making its case? How can we stand up as proud Jews and at the same time keep ourselves safe? How can we possibly fight antisemitism, which can never be defeated but rises in every generation against us?"

The answer is that all this can and must be fought. It is a duty to do so, to stand up for the Jewish people and what they represent, and to fight those who have risen up against the Jews and the West. Giving up is not an option. There are things that can indeed be done to fight this by ordinary Jews, teachers, rabbis, and other community leaders. And there are countless numbers of decent, rational, non-Jews for whom this is very much their fight too. The Jewish people are at the sharp end of all this, but the onslaught against them is the tip of the spear being aimed at civilization itself.

This short book is an attempt to provide a guide to what Jews can all do to mount a resistance against this onslaught. It provides pointers to what they need to understand about the people they're up against and about Israel, Jewish history, and themselves if they are to make a difference. It's a handbook of resilience against a very great evil. It's an attempt to show how the forces of sanity and decency can fight back.

CHAPTER 2
GENERAL PRINCIPLES

• • • •

Before we get down to the details, here are some overarching points to bear in mind.

Is This Book for You?

Emotions in the Jewish community are running very high. If you are someone who wants a physical fistfight with anti-Jewish tormentors, what follows is probably not for you. You'd be better off consulting a martial arts instructor and a lawyer.

If you're someone who really does see this situation as a replay of the 1930s with tragic consequences for Jews who didn't get out in time, then by your own logic it's not worth sticking around to fight the hate in America, Britain, Australia, or any other part of the Jewish diaspora. It's best instead to head for the airport and a new life somewhere else. This book won't help you decide where that may be or whether to make that decision.

If, however, you are frustrated and bewildered, aghast and disbelieving at the malice and derangement unleashed against Israel and the Jews, and you don't want to move to Israel but feel lonely and abandoned and unsure how to behave under this kind of pressure, this book is definitely for you.

If you are someone who thinks this anti-Jewish moment is all Israel's fault because of its government and the way it has behaved, or if you're a left-winger who was knocked sideways by October 7 but are still determined to stick to your left-wing beliefs, please don't think that what follows is not for you because of your assumptions about the book's underlying premises. If you've made it this far, do please read on, as you may be surprised to find things that help you too.

What Are We Facing?

We need to understand, first of all, exactly what we're up against. What the Jewish world has been put through since the October 7 attacks is unique. We can certainly find echoes and precursors in the past, but not in this form and not on this scale.

Antisemitism has always been with us, ever since the Jewish people first emerged some 3,500 years ago. It has taken different forms in every generation—in the ancient Greek and Roman periods, with hostility to the Jews as a people apart; in the medieval period, as a religion that denied Christianity; under the Nazis, as a perceived racial bacillus; and now, in the State of Israel, "the collective Jew" is being viewed as a colonialist interloper. The Jews have been persecuted for being communists and for being capitalists, for being seen as simultaneously all-powerful and as lower than vermin, for being stateless and now for having a state.

All this is known well enough. What's different today is that this venom has burst the boundaries of past horrors to take the war against the Jews onto a different level altogether. The demonization of the Jews today uses tropes straight out of the Nazi playbook; the demonization of Israel uses mind-bending propaganda straight out of Soviet psychological warfare manuals. It's as if, with both the Nazis and the Soviet Union destroyed, they are nevertheless enjoying a posthumous victory that has spread far beyond Germany and the old Soviet bloc to form the default narrative of Jew-hatred among millions throughout the West.

This is, in short, a war that's unlike previous wars and persecutions of the Jews. Hand in glove with the physical war being waged against the Jewish state in the Middle East, this is being waged against Israel and the Jewish world through the collective psyche of the free world. Using techniques of mind control in mainstream and social media and through cultural influencers and the entire humanitarian establishment, the enemies of the Jews have managed to manipulate great swathes of the West—its cultural and political elites, the people who dominate the free world, the privileged classes who educate and mold young people and who make the cultural climate—into a vast global weapon against Israel and the Jews on a battlefield of the mind.

Just as Hamas used the people of Gaza as a weapon of war on the physical battlefield by deploying them as human shields and cannon fodder, so the Western masses have been marshaled in their millions to form a devastating weapon of psychological war against Israel and the Jews. Western Israel–bashers are not just knowingly or unknowingly lending their support to the genocidal Palestinian war against the Jews. They are its invaluable foot soldiers.

That's why Jews are so devastated by what is confronting them, why they feel they're living through a waking nightmare, and why none of this seems to make any sense at all. The "oldest hatred" has once again shifted its shape—but into a form that takes the ineradicable impulse to stick it to the Jews onto a hitherto unthinkable level.

Nor should anyone imagine that, once the drama over the Gaza war has finally subsided, this new and terrifying reality will fade away. Grotesquely, the Palestinian cause has become a meme that repackages in progressive circles otherwise forbidden anti-Jewish bigotry as nothing other than conscience itself.

The emergence of a sectarian Muslim political bloc and "Gaza-first" politicians in Britain, and New York's mayoral election of the Islamist Zohran Mamdani—a man who is reportedly driven by hatred of Israel and the desire to destroy it—means that Jews in Britain and America are increasingly going to feel the heat from a liberal-Islamist alliance that threatens to turn the cause of "Palestine" into the West's second Vietnam.

It's hardly surprising, therefore, that Jewish communities should be so devastated by all this. It's understandable that so many of them feel they're up against forces so vast, so irrational, and so eternal that there's nothing to be done except hunker down and hope the storm bypasses them as individuals.

But it's a counsel of despair that should be resisted. Frightening and discombobulating as this onslaught is, there is plenty that can and should be done to confront it.

To put it another way, failing to do so will not make Jews any safer. Essentially, this campaign is a form of mass bullying. If the victims of bullying are passive and don't react, the bully feels empowered to redouble the attack. Since bullies are basically cowards, if their victims push back the bullies are discouraged from continuing to persecute them. The question is *how* to push back in the most effective and responsible way.

Precisely because this onslaught is so unprecedented, diaspora Jews haven't known how to react. Not surprisingly, therefore, their responses have too often been random, ineffectual, and off base. Faced with an enemy that has been enacting for decades a shrewdly targeted and massively funded strategy of war, waged through Western fellow travelers and useful idiots, the Jewish world has had no strategy at all.

Be Prepared

It's very common for diaspora Jews to feel wholly overwhelmed by all this. The onslaught seems to be as relentless as it is punishing, coming at us from all sides. It's not just the incitement against Israel and the Jews at the street demonstrations, the performative malice on campus, or the poisonous vituperation from the usual suspects in politics on both the left and the right. It's the unending lies from mainstream media outlets, the malicious falsehoods from the entire global humanitarian establishment under the banner of "human rights," and the fact that the calls to murder Israelis, Jews, and Zionists are being made in public without challenge.

All this and more has meant that Jews have felt as if they are being persistently ambushed. Every attack is a shock to the system; those Jews facing personal attacks usually feel caught out on the wrong foot. The bewilderment and distress caused by such encounters are made much worse by a debilitating sense of helplessness, an inability to respond appropriately and adequately, and an uncertainty about how or whether to respond at all.

Such feelings can be significantly remedied by being better prepared. It's essential to think all this through in advance and equip yourself with psychological and verbal weapons *before* the ambush. The first thing to do to prepare yourself is to think about and understand exactly what you're up against.

Dial Down Expectations

To fight back effectively, the Jewish community has to rid itself of certain assumptions. The first is the belief that complaining about antisemitism will bring political and cultural leaders scurrying in righteous outrage to their aid. That rests on the certainty that Jew-hatred is so odious, the irrationality on display so egregious, and the victimization of the Jews so obvious and insupportable that British, Australian, or Canadian government ministers and other authorities will be horrified and jump to the Jews' defense.

This displays an unfortunate failure to grasp the range and depth of the moral and intellectual rot in these purportedly civilized countries. Diaspora Jews need to understand what too many of them have either failed to notice or seek to deny—the collapse of education and the ability to think, the denial of objective truth and its replacement by subjective emotion, the substitution of power for conscience and morality, and the embrace of unhinged, anti-Jewish, Muslim narratives that have capitalized on the implosion of rationality and conscience in the West.

These trends aren't confined to a fringe. They have become mainstream. While there is inevitably less media coverage whenever Israeli military activity is reduced—and therefore fewer lies and incitement being pumped into the public domain—this poisonous genie can't be put back into the bottle.

The period following the October 7 atrocities revealed that a fundamental boundary line in the West has now been broken. The West has lost its moral compass. That's a large part of the reason it has picked on Israel and the Jews—the people who created the moral codes of the West—and their Jewish state that embodies the principles the West now forgets, denies, or seeks to obliterate.

As a result, we Jews must stop expecting people to like us. With a few very honorable exceptions, no one will come to the aid of the Jewish people. Other than President Donald Trump's America, it hasn't happened so far–although there is some worrying indifference or antagonism even among Trump supporters–and it's vanishingly unlikely to happen any time soon. We will have to extricate ourselves from this morass pretty much alone.

What happened after the October 7 atrocities signified a rupture in the moral fabric of the West, an indication that Western civilization is in acute and possibly terminal trouble. It won't recover unless it starts protecting Israel and the Jewish people instead of regarding them as evil, a nuisance, or irrelevant. The West won't do that unless it decides not to commit cultural suicide but instead to recover its historic moral and intellectual core—a core that, not coincidentally, consists of values that originated in Judaism.

The Jewish people must stop expecting to win the argument. The best we can hope to achieve, in a Western world gripped by inexorable decline, is to open the shutters a crack to allow a chink of light to penetrate the darkness—to introduce at least a tiny seed of doubt into the minds of the Israel bashers in the hope that this will grow into a connection with reality.

To equip yourself properly for this task, however, you yourself must have no doubt in your own mind. Doubt is a killer.

That's why it's a remarkably effective weapon to use against your opponent but equally can be a weapon that will undermine *you*. You must be sure of your ground; you must be absolutely certain that you are in the right and not, as the Jews are being painted, supporting wrongdoing. That's why it's so important that you are well informed, even if you never have to use all the information at your disposal.

Is Antisemitism the Same as Anti-Zionism?

The first thing to sort out in your mind is the whole antisemitism/anti-Zionism thing. To do that, you need to take a step back and understand what antisemitism actually is.

It's not just a prejudice. It's not just a form of racism. It's not just an expression of objectionable views about a people called the Jews. It is unique to the Jews. There is no other bigotry like it. That's because it rests on assumptions that are so deranged it amounts to a form of mental disorder. These assumptions involve a paranoid, conspiratorial belief that the Jews have some kind of otherworldly power over global events, they exercise a manipulative, diabolical control over governments and financial and cultural institutions to serve their own interests, and they are uniquely responsible for all the ills of the world. No other group of people, however much they may be the victim of hatred or bigotry, is subjected to this pathologically unhinged attitude.

We know that antisemitism is always with us; it's protean, taking different forms in different situations. And the anti-Israel, anti-Zionist narrative is undoubtedly, at base, virulently anti-Jew.

But Surely, They're as Different as Night and Day?

No. Maybe you can make that distinction at a linguistics seminar, but not in the world of practical, historical, and Jewish reality. It's essential to understand why this is the case so that you can store these arguments in your mental and psychological armory.

There are three reasons. First, the vast majority of Jews support Israel and consider themselves, consequently, to be Zionists.

Second, the demonization of Israel and Zionism displays exactly the same characteristics as antisemitism throughout the ages. Both involve obsessive and deranged lies and blood libels; holding Israel to a higher standard than any other people, or indeed to an utterly impossible standard; the conviction that Israel has unique power in the world; and the belief that it is a diabolical, manipulative, conspiratorial force acting as a hidden hand over world events. All these demonic fantasies singling out Israel as a unique force for bad are characteristics of historic Jew-hatred in its various manifestations.

Third, and most important, even though Zionism as a political movement was created in the nineteenth century, it is an integral part of Judaism itself. Judaism is a unique fusion of the people, the religion, and the land. It holds that the Jews (the people) have a sacred duty imposed upon them by God to live by a set of divinely ordained precepts (the religion) within the patch of earth that the Almighty chose for them (the land of Israel).

That doesn't mean you have to be religiously observant or a Zionist to be a Jew. But it does mean that the presence of the Jewish people as a holy nation in the land of Israel—known in religious language as Zion—is what Judaism is all about, and the yearning to return to the land is integral to Jewish history, thought, and prayer. It's like a three-legged stool. Knock out the

Zionism leg and the stool falls over. That's why an attack on Israel's existence is an attack on Judaism itself.

No other faith, people, or nationality has this multi-faceted character. It's another thing that makes the Jewish people unique. And it's the feature that non-Jews find so difficult to grasp and leads to endless misunderstanding. People wonder why the Jews are even entitled to have a country of their own since Judaism is "just another religion." Well, Judaism isn't "just" anything. It's uniquely and inextricably multidimensional. It involves faith, peoplehood, and nationhood. And that needs to be unpacked and explained, not least to many Jews themselves.

So, Everyone Telling Lies About Israel Is an Antisemite, Right?

Wrong. There's a distinction to be drawn between people and the prejudice. The fact that anti-Zionism is a form of antisemitism doesn't mean that everyone holding these views about Israel is an antisemite. They may merely be people who are totally ignorant about Jews, Judaism, and the Middle East, and who, as a result of being bombarded day in and day out with lies about Israel and its Arab persecutors, have swallowed these views whole.

Unsurprisingly, such people don't take kindly to being called an antisemite. They are potentially open to having at least some of their preconceptions about Jews, Judaism, or Israel challenged and even changed for the better. It's advisable not to turn them off by an insult that really may be way off base.

Park the Antisemitism Thing

There's also no point thinking, "Oh well, what's going on is just antisemitism, so we have no alternative but to keep our heads down because antisemitism is profoundly irrational, and it's therefore impossible to argue with antisemites." This is a recipe for despair. It's also a deeply unhelpful generalization.

The first thing to bear in mind is that it's extremely inadvisable to level the charge of antisemitism at anyone who's telling lies about Israel. It may make you feel better to do so, but it doesn't get you anywhere.

Some of these attackers are indeed dyed-in-the-wool Jew-haters. If someone really is an antisemite, however, the charge may bounce straight off them. They may not understand that vicious tropes about Jews, such as the claim that they control the world through devious means or that they kill people to harvest their internal organs, are indeed examples of antisemitism.

That's because, astonishingly, some people believe such things to be true. Such real antisemites may therefore bat away the accusation of antisemitism as merely a self-serving and meaningless insult.

However, even if people are spewing lies about Israel which meet the definition of antisemitism, they still might not be antisemites.

Here's an example of the distinctions that need to be drawn:

"The UK is occupied and controlled by Jewish supremacy" is an unvarnished, paranoid, antisemitic libel against British Jews. This statement was made by Dr. Rahmeh Aladwan, a self-described British-Palestinian doctor in Britain who, at the time of writing this, has been suspended[2] while under investigation by the General Medical Council for this and other antisemitic comments.[3]

"Israel is willfully killing civilians in Gaza." That's a libel about Israel that is the opposite of the truth. As the military analyst John Spencer has written, the Israel Defense Forces (IDF) went to greater lengths in the Gaza war than any other army in the world to avoid killing civilians.[4] To minimize civilian casualties, the IDF made phone calls and sent text messages to civilians residing in buildings designated for attack.[5] It also repeatedly moved the civilian population to "safe zones" in Gaza away from the fighting.[6]

The claim that Israel willfully killed civilians is not only the opposite of the truth. It is also fundamentally antisemitic because such reverse-truth claims are made about Israel alone. Only Israel is subjected to a nonstop campaign of demonization and delegitimization based on lies. But the people articulating it may believe firmly that it's true simply because the BBC or *The New York Times* has told them so.

There's another reason why it's inadvisable to use the term "antisemitism" at all when it comes to attacks on Israel. This is that it's been made almost unsayable because of the widespread belief, fueled by the lunacy of current discourse about Israel, that the Jews use it as a shield behind which to hide the crimes of the Jewish state. Of course, one could well say that this charge is itself antisemitic, but that isn't very constructive or realistic either. The fact is that when the "*a*-word" is used, it shuts down discourse, leaving issues not only unaddressed but overlaid with a resentment that the word was deployed at all.

At the core of this resentment lurks an even more terrible fact—that for many in the West, the Jews alone can never be viewed as victims. This is obviously absurd, since the Jews are the most persecuted people in history.

That, however, is precisely the point. The persecution of the Jews is an ineradicable stain on the West's own history. In particular, the West's complicity in the Nazi Holocaust—by creating over many centuries the culture that incubated its genocidal agenda against the Jewish people, by appeasing Hitler until it was too late, and by closing their borders against the desperate Jews, thus sealing their fate in the Nazi death trap—has created in the Western psyche an intolerable sense of guilt.

The way the West chooses to deal with this is by denying that Jews can be victims targeted for attack simply because they are Jews and instead holds them responsible for the terrible things that happen to them.

That's one reason why the West refuses to acknowledge the Palestinian Arab agenda of extermination against them, claiming instead that the Israelis are the oppressors of the Palestinian Arabs. It's why people tore down the publicly displayed posters of the Israeli babies and the children, women, and men who were kidnapped into Gaza after the October 7 attack. It's why Westerners accuse Israelis of being Nazis, to diminish the unique evil of the Nazis and thus wipe out the West's own guilt over being accessories to the Holocaust.

Worse still, many also believe that the Jews claim antisemitism as a shield to conceal the purported crimes not just of Israel but of the Jewish people themselves who—in the fevered imagination of the Jew-haters—are busily manipulating the world for their own benefit.

Many people also firmly believe that anti-Zionism has nothing to do with antisemitism. As discussed earlier, that is profoundly misguided. It's an argument that may be worth having in the right circumstances, but it's complicated and needs to be handled with care. The resentment against the charge of antisemitism is itself deeply antisemitic. But there's no point in needlessly stirring this particular can of worms. There are plenty of telling and important points you can and should make without throwing around accusations of antisemitism.

Don't Get Emotional, Get Smart

When confronted with vicious prejudice against Israel and an apparently total resistance to evidence and reason, a number of quite overwhelming emotions may well rise up inside you. Fury is one: deep anger at the sheer unfairness and injustice of what's being said. Disbelief is another: you can't believe that someone you thought was a normal, sensible person has turned out to hold views that aren't just malevolent but crazy. A third is fear, because not so far below the surface of these obsessional and paranoid views lies the desire to just get rid of these troublesome Jews. And a fourth, perhaps most overwhelming of all, is shock, upset, disorientation, and a quite devastating feeling of loneliness.

It's very hard to keep such emotions under control. There may be an immediate instinct to lash out, to hit back. However, "How dare you speak about us like that!" is the wrong response. If you even think it, stop that thought as fast as possible. It's not a smart thought. It makes you emotional, and you'll lose the argument immediately—not to mention cause yourself distress and leave you frustrated that you've let them get away with it.

More importantly, it places you on the territory that your tormentors have themselves created, which is paved with their own warped thinking. It forces you to play defense, responding in effect to a "when did you stop beating your wife" kind of question. In other words, no matter what you say, you've lost the initiative and the argument from the start.

So don't go there. Treat the barb or the troubling behavior not so much as an affront but as an opportunity. Use it to respond with what *you* want to put out there. Turn it around so that you take the initiative and place in front of your antagonist some information they're not expecting and will never have heard before.

So, for example, if someone is wearing a Palestine pin or is holding a Palestine flag in order to go to a demonstration, you might say, "Wow, I'm really surprised you're wearing/carrying a terrorist symbol. I thought you opposed violence/were a Quaker/ supported dialogue and peace?"

Perhaps the pin or flag bearer might respond, "This isn't a terrorist flag; it's the flag of Palestine."

To which you might say, "Actually, it has a fascinating history. Let me tell you about it. See the color combination of black, green, and white, with a red triangle? That first emerged in 1916 as the symbol of the Arab Revolt against the Ottoman Empire, which ruled this whole area. Yes, really, Islamic imperialists! The symbol was then adopted by the Palestine Liberation Organization (PLO) when it was created as a terrorist group in 1964. And guess what—when the terrorist PLO was renamed the Palestinian Authority in 1993, this terrorist flag was also rebranded as the flag of Palestine."

The beauty of this kind of response is that it flatters the other person's intelligence by telling them an obscure fact that very few others will know. At the same time, it slips into their mind the otherwise distinctly unwelcome idea that they're carrying or wearing a terrorist symbol. Once planted, that thought can just sit in their mind. Maybe it won't have any effect at all. But maybe it might just plant a seed of doubt about the position they're taking.

Do You Engage or Do You Hide?

This kind of exchange, however, raises a much broader question about the dilemma that faces every Jewish person confronted by anti-Israel or anti-Jewish behavior. Do you choose to engage with the individual or institution that's behaved in an offensive or threatening way, or do you take the path of least resistance? This worries a lot of people because there's no easy or obvious answer. Either way, it involves both an upside and a downside.

Engaging may well be unpleasant, distressing, or even frightening. It may carry a risk of escalation into an aggressive or violent response. It may also lead to the rupture of a professional, academic, or business relationship, or the end of a friendship.

Many have concluded, therefore, that engaging with the offending party is a relatively pointless gesture that's likely to bring few benefits. Your antagonist is unlikely to be persuaded or defeated, while there's a distinct possibility that you may instead do yourself significant harm. The sensible goal then, as this thinking goes, is to get through your studies, conclude your business deal, or continue to have a pleasant and civil working relationship with your colleagues.

Others, though, have a very different attitude to this. They regard it almost as a sacred duty to engage with such opponents in whatever way seems appropriate, either by verbal confrontation and argument or, in the case of institutional prejudice, using complaints, procedures, or legal action to force them to back down. They believe it is a betrayal of the Jewish people not to uphold Israel's case and thus fail to challenge the lies, bigotry, or discrimination. They don't want to be "Jews with trembling knees" who keep their heads well below the parapet at all times.

There is surely no single answer to this dilemma. It all depends on the circumstances and, no less crucially, on the individual Jewish person's temperament and personality. Some situations may be difficult but not career ending; others may expose the Jewish challenger to a constant but unnervingly concealed process of attrition and undermining. Some people are outward going and confident, relishing a combative challenge and able to handle any flak that may come their way. Others are quiet and inward, lacking the self-confidence to take on a potentially threatening situation.

People need to decide how to behave in accordance not just with the specific circumstances but also with their own attributes and limitations.

However, those who decide to keep their heads down and avoid any altercation may well find that this leaves them with a permanent sense of regret and even failure—not so much because of any criticism they may encounter from more robust acquaintances, but more from a sense of a lost opportunity that they wish they had taken. They may come to feel they haven't done justice to the Jewish part of themselves, which they may realize too late is more important to them than they had imagined.

That would be unfortunate. So, it's probably wise to try to strike some kind of balance appropriate to the circumstances, in which the victimized Jew at least does enough to feel that personal honor has been satisfied in some way while not engaging in the kind of high-profile confrontation that others may relish.

Tactical Preparation: Different Audiences

Jews are facing overt Jew-hatred or hostile confrontations over Israel in a wide variety of situations. Every one of these involves a different dynamic requiring an approach tailored to that situation. There's no single template for approaching these difficult encounters. What may work in one set of circumstances may be wildly inappropriate for another.

Here are some of the most obvious and common potential battlegrounds:

- Politicians, media, and other cultural players and arenas
- Social media
- Anti-Israel hate marches and demonstrations
- Students and faculty on university campuses
- Colleagues in the workplace
- Friends and acquaintances
- Family members
- Other faith members: Christians and Muslims
- The far left and the far right

All these situations require thought and discernment. When asking yourself, "What should I do: fight, persuade, or disengage?" first make a judgment about whether your opponent is a hopeless case or not.

Of course, you can't know the answer to that for certain. Even if such individuals were to come out with a grotesque libel against Israel, they may just be parroting what they've heard on social media or in their peer group. That doesn't necessarily mean their mind is closed.

But if they were to use one of the ancient libels of Jew-hatred, such as "the Jews are killing the Palestinians just as they killed

Christ," or "the Talmud teaches Jews to cheat non-Jews out of their money," it's a fair bet that you're not going to get anywhere through reason and persuasion. So your wisest course is to put some distance between such individuals and yourself as fast as possible.

Understand Your Enemy

True antisemites like this are hopeless cases. Ideologues, whether from the left or the right, aren't necessarily hopeless, but they are certainly very difficult and pose particular but different challenges, which we'll look at a little later. The middle ground provides much more promising opportunities, but this still needs to be thought through properly beforehand to avoid making false and unhelpful assumptions.

For starters, you may not realize they are indeed from a "middle ground" if what they're saying sounds to your ears angry or extreme. But if they're not left- or right-wing ideologues or religious fanatics, who are all signed up to inflexible dogmas, then chances are that they're part of the huge army of what are ungenerously called "useful idiots."

Classically, these are well-meaning naïfs who know precious little about the Jews or the Middle East but have been enraged by the story they've assimilated of Palestinian wretchedness and Israeli perfidy. Don't assume these individuals are necessarily bad or dumb.

Understand instead that what drives them may well be admirable feelings: compassion for victims and the vulnerable, a passion for justice, and a hatred of oppressive power. It's just that they assume Israel is on the wrong side of all those good things and "Palestine" is on the right side. And that's because the entire cultural discourse from those in public life who they believe are well-informed people of integrity, such as human rights lawyers, the UN, or doctors serving in Gaza, continuously feeds them this narrative with virtually no public pushback based on the facts.

It's obviously a pretty steep challenge to reverse that fixed belief in their minds. In order to stand a chance of denting the opinionated armor of any member of such groups, you need to understand where that individual is coming from—who or what is behind what that individual believes, what's driving those forces in turn, and the often jaw-droppingly unholy alliances that have been formed between them.

Here are some of those unholy alliances that will have produced the viciously anti-Israel or anti-Jewish mindset that confronts you, alliances over which you may understandably be bamboozled:

- Anti-West revolutionaries and Muslim jihadists
- Left-wingers, Islamists, and white supremacists
- MAGA isolationists and the revolutionary left
- "Queers for Palestine"
- Climate change activists and Palestinian Arabs
- Progressive Christian churches and the Islamic world
- Progressive Jews and the Islamic world

You may well be baffled by these alliances. "Queers for Palestine"? *Seriously*? Even though homosexuals in Palestinian Arab society would typically be shot or thrown to their death from rooftops simply for being gay?

MAGA conservatives, who are viscerally opposed to progressive politics, making common cause with Marxist radicals or liberal universalists?

Jews—who, according to Islamic sacred texts, must be wiped off the face of the earth or else treated as an inferior caste—cozying up to Islamic extremists and pretending that Islamophobia, which silences all mention of rampant Muslim antisemitism, is the equivalent of antisemitism?

Christians—whose fellow worshippers are being slaughtered by Islamists in their tens of thousands, getting burned alive in Nigerian churches, and are being subjected to an attempt to eradicate them from the face of the earth—lining up with the Islamic world against Israel, the only country in the Middle East that guarantees Christians freedom of worship and full civil rights?

What links these unlikely allies to each other is their shared loathing of Jews, or a mutual sense of pathological alienation and resentment, or their common aim of overturning Western civilization and replacing it by an entirely new world. The fact that the precise type of new world may be radically different from and indeed inimical to the one envisaged on other agendas is for these purposes irrelevant. These are alliances of convenience, each of them ignoring the issues that in different circumstances might bring them to blows. Instead, they are using each other to reach their revolutionary or exterminatory goal.

So, if you find yourself confronted by a gay person accusing Israel rather than Hamas or Iran of "homophobia," a Trump supporter declaring that Israel's creation in 1948 was "a mistake," or a Christian telling you that Islam is the "religion of peace," don't allow yourself to be sidetracked and knocked off course by the bizarre contradictions.

Such Christians and Muslims are motivated at root by theological Jew-hatred. Left-wing ideologues, including climate change activists, are driven by hatred of Western capitalism and its supposedly "Jewish roots." "Queers for Palestine," along with "trans activists" and "anti-racists" demanding penance for "whiteness"—who are in fact racially prejudiced against white people—subscribe to "intersectionality," the doctrine of intersecting oppressions.

This derives from the Marxist division of the world into the powerful, who can never do anything good, and the powerless, who can never do anything bad. Under this doctrine, the Palestinian Arabs, who are deemed to be powerless, can never do anything bad while the Jews, who are deemed to be all-powerful, can never be victims.

Ultra-right-wing MAGA conspiracy theorists, who are on the opposite side of the political spectrum, are characterized by an incoherent ideology that springs not from any rational thought process but from a toxic cocktail of rage and resentment and is overwhelmingly driven by hatred and fear of Jews.

These various motivations all devolve into one common position: the hatred of Zionism and the Jews and the belief that the world would be a better place if Israel ceased to exist.

Understand where they're all coming from in order to respond appropriately. Some specific suggestions about how to do so will follow later.

CHAPTER 3

LET'S GET DOWN TO SOME SPECIFICS

• • • •

Stop Playing Defense

In order to fight back, Israel's supporters and the Jewish world need to change their entire approach. They must get off the back foot and onto the front foot; they must stop playing defense and go on the offense instead.

That doesn't mean they should be offensive. It means they need to adjust their thinking from trying to make the case that Israel is innocent of the charges being laid against it to an approach that focuses instead on the behavior and attitudes of the other side.

Of course, Israel's case should be made. In the right circumstances, it's essential that people should become educated and informed about the truth of Israel's position and behavior. But we're dealing with a state of affairs that isn't normal. Language has been hijacked, no dissent is permitted, and minds have been fried.

As a result, there are many situations where educating opponents on the facts about Israel and the Middle East will fall on totally deaf ears. Such foes simply don't want to hear Israel's side of things, they don't want to hear about the justice of Israel's cause, and they certainly don't want to hear that the behavior of the Israel Defense Forces (IDF) is morally upstanding. So, if its supporters protest that Israel is the victim rather than the aggressor in the Middle East, there will be a loud sound of minds snapping shut as Israel's opponents roll their eyes and dismiss this as Zionist propaganda.

Playing defense is a mug's game because it invariably means engaging with your opponents on territory that they themselves have mapped out as the grounds for prosecution in the kangaroo court of received opinion. Israel's defenders therefore find themselves protesting: "No, we're not committing genocide/starving civilians/deliberately killing babies/stealing other people's land/ breaking international law."

You will not only never win that argument, but you will never even get a hearing while you are engaging with these foes on their terms. The way they frame their attack makes it impossible to do so because a wholly preposterous premise, which all these accusations are, is innately unanswerable. The Jewish world has been trying to answer these preposterously unanswerable accusations for decades—and then wonders why it keeps losing.

The proper strategy, the way to gain these foes' attention, is to put *them* on the defensive. Israel's supporters need to move from their implicit protest, "Why are you being so unfair to us?" to the implicit charge, "You are betraying everything you claim to stand for." If their armor is to be dented, the enemies of Israel and the Jews have to be challenged on their own grounds of justice and conscience and be revealed instead as standing for everything they claim to despise.

The Jewish world needs to map out its own ground proactively, not least by reclaiming the language. It needs to take the argument to its foes *before* they launch their own attack and to do so independently of whatever these opponents are saying. It needs to address its tormentors on terms that matter to and have meaning for *them*. To be on target and frame its responses appropriately, it needs to think through where these opponents are coming from. And in certain circumstances, it needs to hold their feet to the fire in a way the defensive, parapet-ducking diaspora Jews almost never do.

Above all, the Jewish world must develop an actual strategy. Astoundingly, neither community leaders nor individuals actually have one. Instead, they reel from one side of the ring to the other as they take punch after punch to the collective Jewish head, lashing out in response with wild jabs that fail to land a decisive blow and often miss their target altogether. They are always reactive. They have never worked out a strategy to take the fight to the enemy instead.

Safety

For individuals, there's a delicate line to be trodden between taking the path of least resistance and standing up for the Jewish people. The absolute priority, however, is to keep yourself physically safe. Be alert and keep up with developments in your own country, in Israel, and in Europe so that you become aware of potential dangers ahead. Don't pick fights that are obvious you can't win. If you are fit enough, learn Krav Maga, the self-defense system that uses techniques drawn from aikido, boxing, judo, karate, and wrestling. And develop the non-martial arts equivalent to Krav Maga, a system of fighting back that draws upon your personal armory of mouth and brain.

You may not think you possess such an armory. You do. It's just a question of how best to deploy it.

Your Feelings

You need to look after yourself in other ways, too. Understand you are not alone. Make sure you don't feel as if you are. Isolation is the first cousin to demoralization and defeat.

You feel alone because of the deafening, wall-to-wall hatred and lies about Israel which assail you every day and from all sides. You feel as if you and maybe a very small band of like-minded friends or relatives are the only ones confronting an entire global establishment telling you that you are at best deluded and at worst actively supporting evil.

This isn't true. Countless numbers of people think and feel very much as you do. Many beyond the Jewish community are decent, sensible people who admire Israel and the Jews. They understand the extent to which the media and cultural establishments are not only regurgitating murderous lies but appear to have lost altogether their ability to reason and to process factual information.

They, too, are aghast and shocked by all this. They may not know much about Jews or the Middle East, but they recognize self-serving nonsense when they hear it and recoil from disorder and intimidation when they see them. They're also observing with great concern the rising power of predatory, jihadi Islam on the streets and in their neighborhoods—in America as well as in Britain, which is much further down that particular road to cultural extinction—and they understand that Israel's battle is their own battle too.

In London, as the war in Gaza ground agonizingly on and the streets were convulsed by anti-Israel hate marches, a non-Jewish taxi driver eyed his Jewish passenger in his rearview mirror and said, "We're all with you, you know." To which the passenger replied, "Thank you; but I wish I could believe that." The taxi driver then stopped his cab, twisted around in his seat, and told the passenger, face to face, "We *are* all with you. You've got to believe it."

The Jewish passenger is a friend of mine who told me about this encounter. A tiny anecdote, perhaps. But once you start listening for such people, you start to realize you aren't alone at all. There are millions who grasp that their Western identity itself is now in a state of crisis from a collapse of cultural self-belief and their leaders' passive acquiescence to their nations' creeping takeover by jihadi Islam. That "silent majority" is now voting in droves for "populist" leaders who promise to give their country and its future back to them.

Those millions are themselves defamed as "racists" by the same "progressives" who are in the forefront of demonizing Israel with anti-Jewish tropes. If you are a liberal Jew, however, the backing and support for Israel and the Jewish people coming from people who are in revolt against mass immigration and Islamization may be of scant comfort if you believe that those positions are beyond the pale.

But the image of such people as racist, thuggish, uneducated knuckle-draggers who hate all immigrants and foreigners is very far from the truth. Some are like that; the vast majority, however, are not. They are people with a moral compass and a firm grip on reality. If you sat down with them, you might like them!

If you are perplexed by the defamatory way in which Israel has been presented by cultural leaders, it may help you understand this if you realize that *all* who challenge any liberal shibboleths get the same vicious treatment.

It's so much easier to fight back if you realize that you are not alone. The backing of decent, balanced, grounded people makes us all braver.

Of course, everyone needs to find their own balance between engaging and hiding. Not everyone is temperamentally cut out to march onto this battlefield. But whether you engage with these hostile forces or decide to keep a low profile, the combination of this demonization with the devastating trauma experienced by Israelis—whose loved ones have been murdered, maimed, tortured, or fallen in battle, whose minds as well as bodies have been shattered, and whose families have been torn apart—has inflicted a very heavy toll on many diaspora Jews whose deep connections with Israel have meant the trauma has been shared.

It's important therefore to protect yourself against this as much as you can to avoid succumbing to panic, depression, or despair. Learn to tune out the noise. The mainstream media, with its systemic malice and falsehoods about Israel, has both a corrupting and a lowering effect: corrupting because its monocultural message makes people believe the lies, and lowering because the lies carry the insidious and not-so-subliminal message that the Jews are the problem—that *you* are the problem.

You are not. Israel is not. You've got to believe it.

Social media, which can provide a corrective to this false messaging, also spews out an unstoppable geyser of venom against Israel and the Jews. In addition, it tends to act like a drug, addicting you to the torrent of tweets and posts that bring you yet another development, yet another outrageous comment, yet another set of responses. This is unhealthy because it can quickly overwhelm you and distort your perspective.

So, discipline yourself to limit your use of social media. Don't dwell on atrocities; try not to look at the snuff videos of Islamist depravity that lurk on X and can dangerously lower your resilience by close exposure to such unalloyed evil and the suffering it causes. Avoid being sucked into vicious spats on X with unhinged and hateful individuals. Limit or, better still, cancel altogether your exposure to the most vicious media outlets such as *The New York Times,* MSNBC, the BBC, or Britain's Sky News.

Limit your exposure to images of Israeli suffering; restrict also your exposure to both online sources and personal acquaintances that transmit a relentless message of pessimism and catastrophe. Train yourself to balance every one of these with something positive about the world. If you think that just sounds too fanciful or Pollyannaish, then you've already got a problem. There are *always* good things happening, in your own life and in the world around you. And there are huge positives about Judaism and Israel. Remind yourself constantly that the Jews are the eternal people and that every culture that tried to wipe us out has disappeared while the Jewish people have survived and thrived.

And in order to not feel alone, don't be alone. Reach out to others who share your views; join groups and make friendships and alliances, both in person and online. The sense of security, comfort, and consolation that come from surrounding yourself with people who really do have your back can't be exaggerated.

Understand What They Think That's Wrong

It's very important not to engage with the Israel bashers on the hostile grounds they set out. Equally, it's important to acknowledge that it may be productive and necessary to meet them on the grounds that mean a lot to them.

Many of these opponents aren't innately bad people but are being driven by a set of groundless and wrong-headed assumptions.

Behind the specific accusations they hurl against Israel lie the real accusations, a set of underlying assumptions about Israel, Jews, and Judaism that are ignorant, prejudiced, and wrong. These include, for example, the belief that:

- Judaism is merely a religion;
- the Palestinians are indigenous to the land that Israel occupied;
- Israel is a big country, probably the size of France;
- the Jews run the world;
- Zionism only started in the nineteenth century; and
- Israel was only created because the world felt sorry for the Jews after the Holocaust.

You may be burning up with the injustice of these and other falsehoods. You may feel it's intolerable to meet people who think such things even some of the way. You may think the only proper response is to give them a piece of your mind and tell them in no uncertain terms about the error of their beliefs.

Please, park those feelings. Do you just want to feel better yourself by venting? Or do you want to make a difference, however modest? If it's the latter, then you need to deal with your opponents as they are, not how you want to force them to be.

Some, if not many, of these people can potentially be reached through the right kind of approach. That means understanding where they're coming from and tailoring your responses appropriately.

That does not mean going along with the falsehoods they believe. It means instead paying due regard to their dignity and self-respect. It means showing them that you understand that they are motivated by good instincts, which it's important they realize in turn that you share because you are all decent people.

They're going to turn off immediately if you start lecturing them about the history of the Middle East and the way the Jews were repeatedly shafted over their right to the land of Israel. And they certainly don't want to hear that the people they've been supporting for decades are actually genocidal lunatics. Of course, you want them to come to understand this, but you need to employ a circular approach rather than a sledgehammer.

They want to hear about the things that matter to them, such as peace and coexistence. So, tell them about the Arabs who are Israeli citizens. Tell them that more than half of all newly qualified doctors are Israeli Arabs. Tell them about the Israeli Arabs and Druze who have served with heroism and even lost their lives in the IDF fighting for their country, the State of Israel.

Tell them about Lucy Aharish, the Israeli Arab TV presenter who wept on air over the returning Israeli hostages. Tell them the positive things that an increasing number of Israeli Arabs say about the country they live in and about feeling Israeli. Here's an Instagram post by an Israeli Arab Muslim woman who wrote during the October 7 war:

> When you run for shelter in Israel into a syna-
> gogue, and feel this pride of being an Israeli Arab
> Muslim so protected and safe with our Jewish
> family. My Mother Israel, I love you with my
> soul.[7]

Or here's Professor Mouna Maroun, vice president and dean of research at the University of Haifa and the former head of the Sagol Department of Neurobiology. She was the first Israeli Arab woman to hold a senior faculty position in the natural sciences, and in November 2023 she wrote something rather lovely:

> Israeli Arabs and Jews are like salt and pepper: They both belong on the table, and once they're sprinkled into a dish, it's almost impossible to distinguish between them.[8]

Find Common Ground

Try to make common cause wherever you can with people who come out with hostile comments about Israel. For example, you could agree that you are absolutely against racism and oppression. Suggest that, as a result, you might be starting a WhatsApp group to document and bring to public attention the hanging of gay people in Iran, the stoning of women in Sudan, the torture and murder of Palestinian Arabs in Gaza by Hamas, and the incarceration and torture of Palestinian Arab dissidents by the Palestinian Authority in the "West Bank"[9]—and invite your interlocutor to join you in that group.

Find a way of reaching out to such people even over some of their most neuralgic claims. This is obviously not easy, but one way of doing this is by seeking out a detail on which you can agree and then providing an uncontentious but obscure piece of information such as the history of the "Palestine" flag mentioned earlier. This can be disarming, in every sense of the word.

For example, if they say, "Jews are always claiming antisemitism to cover up the crimes of Israel," you might respond by saying, "I'm also fed up with hearing 'antisemitism' all the time. It's a really idiotic word. Did you know it was actually invented by an antisemite? It was a nineteenth century German called Wilhelm Marr who wanted to give hatred of Jews a pseudoscientific gloss by associating it with the bogus racial theories that were thought at the time to be scientific. Isn't it amazing how many people are taken in by totally rubbish claims just because the people making them sound impressive!"

Be Positive

Try to introduce Israel into public discourse in positive ways. Call into radio shows and say something nice about Israel, however trivial. Show your non-Jewish neighbors your holiday video filmed in Eilat or Tel Aviv. Play Israeli and Jewish music at a party. Show that you are proud of both Israel and being Jewish; wear something that does so in a way that people will find intriguing rather than confrontational.

An American acquaintance wears a wristband she had made in Israel's colors of blue and white, which is imprinted with Hebrew words. On one side, they form a saying from the Talmud: "For my sake the world was created." And on the other, a phrase from the Book of Genesis: "I am but dust and ashes."

On the New York subway, she was confronted by a woman who asked aggressively if the wristband had anything to do with Israel. The wristband wearer said it did and told the woman what the words meant, explaining that they conveyed the permanent tension in Judaism between man's significance and insignificance. The challenger's aggression melted away, and she said she found that really interesting and went away thinking something positive rather than negative about Jews.

An enterprising and energetic Jewish anti-hate warrior, Eitan Chitayat, has developed a grassroots viral campaign called, "I'm That Jew."[10] It's a deceptively simple idea: Jewish people are invited to say what kind of Jew they are in a word or phrase. Thus not only, perhaps, "I'm that shy Jew," "I'm that hopeful Jew," or "I'm that always-writing Jew," but also, "I'm that hang-in-there-and-hold-your-head-up Jew," "I'm that always-trying-to-make-things-just-a-little-better Jew," and "I'm that whatever-mood-I'm-in-the-mood-to-be Jew." In other words, he raps with thoughts, images, characteristics, foibles, wishes and fears, and hangs the word "Jew" on them to normalize, demystify, and detoxify the word.

He creates very short videos on Instagram around the theme. He produces T-shirts, hoodies, and mugs with "I'm That Jew" emblazoned upon them. He distributes stickers in different colors saying, "I'm That Jew." His website says it's about "Jewish people owning who we are and celebrating that. Openly."

This produces two enormous advantages. It encourages Jewish pride and confidence in the person wearing the T-shirt or distributing the stickers. And it transforms the image of Jews among the general public from one characterized by harmful stereotypes and lies to something that tells people Jews are as diverse as the rest of humanity, and all in a quirky, amusing, and endearing way.

The reaction he gets from the general public, he says, is overwhelmingly positive. People are interested, intrigued, and entertained. What he demonstrates above all is that to fight the hate, Jews have to be braver, more out there, not "hiding-their-light-under-a-bushel Jews," but "look-this-is-who-we-are Jews." They need to have the confidence about being Jews themselves to transmit that glow to others. You fight hate by asserting yourself against it. If you react to hate by internalizing it and hiding, the haters have won.

Reframe the Narrative

For decades, the Jewish world allowed its enemies to frame the narrative. They hijacked language and weaponized the West's post-truth, post-moral culture to push their agenda that Israel and the Jews were on the wrong side of everything that was good and just because of their "oppression" of the Palestinian Arabs and "occupation" of their land.

The world was made to believe that peace and justice hinged on "the Palestinians": that unless they had a state of their own (whether alongside Israel or instead of Israel was never entirely clear) there would be no solution to the Middle East conflict. Justice for the Palestinians was deemed to be the issue that drove all before it. By apparently denying that outcome, Israel came to be perceived as the enemy of humanity itself. The Palestinians were the big issue. The Arab and Muslim world couldn't reconcile itself to the West because their plight remained unresolved. Israel was the big problem.

It was the Big Lie. But the Jewish world never identified it as such and never fought it. It never sought to seize back control of that narrative. Instead, it went along with it—appeasing it, shaving off its most dangerous edges, but with too many Jews themselves falling for at least parts of the lie. The terrible onslaught against Israel and the Jews following the October 7 atrocities is a direct result of that egregious failure by the Jewish world.

But, as a result of that explosion of aggression, there's now ironically an opportunity to seize back control of the narrative and reframe it in the interests of both Israel and the truth. With the smoke of the Middle East battlefield not yet cleared, we can nevertheless already see that Israel is not the problem but the solution to the most pressing issue being faced by the West—the march against it of predatory Islam, the very force against which Israel itself has been battling.

Britain is beginning to wake up at last to the reality of Islamization, and America—where this process is not as far advanced but is nevertheless making steady inroads—needs to do so more than it has done. As this problem becomes ever more pronounced, it will become increasingly clear that Israel is not just holding the line for the West in the Middle East itself but is battling the very same Islamist forces that are now achieving critical mass in the West and increasingly threaten its identity and way of life.

If the Gulf States and the Muslim world finally make peace with Israel, the Palestinian issue will be over. Israel will become the fulcrum of an arc of prosperity in the Middle East, while Britain and America increasingly succumb to domination by the Islamists whom the West has so unwisely embraced while dumping on Israel.

Even if the war to destroy the Jewish state continues to roil the region, Israel is not the problem but the solution. That's the message the Jewish world should be pushing at every opportunity to reframe the narrative.

Reclaim the Hijacked Language

An important part of reframing the narrative is to reclaim language that has been hijacked. There are words such as "antisemitism" that have become almost impossible to utter because they produce a hostile reaction. There are words such as "Zionism" that have become toxic and have been turned from neutral descriptors into a badge of shame. There are other words such as "genocide" whose meaning has been turned inside out.

Fighting back means restoring the truthful meaning of words, turning their toxicity into a boomerang against those who have used them as weapons to harm the Jewish people, and deploying other words, phrases, and word associations as weapons of truth against the campaign of lies.

Antisemitism

Let's start with "antisemitism." As previously noted, it's a nonsense word invented by someone who hated Jews and Judaism. It has also lost much of its power because the anti-Israel agenda has successfully framed it as a shield wielded by Israel's defenders to sanitize its supposed crimes.

But the reason it's become almost unsayable is that the West wants to erase the notion of Jewish victimization because it can't deal with its implications. That's something that must be resisted.

So, wherever possible, antisemitism should be replaced by terms such as "Jew-hatred," "Jew-baiting," "Jew-hunting," "anti-Jewish bullying," "Judeophobia," or even invented phrases such as "Judaism derangement syndrome." The obvious difficulty is that these are all inelegant and awkward terms, and it's impossible to avoid using "antisemitism" in some circumstances. But introducing such alternatives would help.

Genocide

As well as defending Israel against grotesquely inverted charges such as genocide or ethnic cleansing, let's use such words and phrases correctly to describe the people who really are guilty of such behavior. Genocide is the intentional extermination of a country or a people, in whole or in part. Since Iran, Hamas, and the wider Palestinian Islamist movement aim to exterminate Israel and kill every Jew—as their religious and political leaders have repeatedly told us—they should always be described as "genocidal."

Here are some of the things they have said that demonstrate this:

- On January 15, 2001, at a meeting with organizers of the International Conference for Support of the Intifada, Iran's Supreme Leader Ayatollah Ruhollah Khomeini stated: "The foundation of the Islamic regime is opposition to Israel and the perpetual subject of Iran is the elimination of Israel from the region."[11]

- On September 2, 2010, Iran's current Supreme Leader, Ayatollah Ali Khamenei, said: "Israel is a hideous entity in the Middle East which will undoubtedly be annihilated".[12]

- In 2002, Hezbollah's leader Hassan Nasrallah said the fact that all the Jews were banded together in Israel made it possible to fight them when grouped together and saved the trouble of chasing them around the world.[13]

- In July 2019, a senior Hamas official, Fathi Hammad, called on Palestinians living around the world to "go out and slaughter and kill Jews." Warning that the blockade on the Gaza Strip must be lifted, he said Palestinians "must attack every Jew who exists in the globe, slaughter and kill them." [14]

- In 2009, the internal order document of the Sixth Fatah General Conference in Bethlehem declared, "The armed popular revolution is the only inevitable way to the liberation of Palestine," and added that, "The struggle will not end until the elimination of the Zionist entity and the liberation of Palestine."[15]

The word "genocide" has been systematically repeated in conjunction with Israel in order to cement that grotesque and mendacious association into people's minds. The same hyphenated tactic should be regularly employed by talking about "genocidal Iran," "genocidal Hamas," or the "genocidal Palestinians" to cement the truth into their minds instead.

Colonialism

Israel is accused of being colonialist. That's because it's thought to be occupying land that belongs to the Palestinians. This is the reverse of the truth.

The right of the Jewish people alone to restore their ancient home in the land of Israel was established by the Great Powers at the San Remo conference in 1920 and by the League of Nations in the 1922 Mandate for Palestine. This represented the international community's legally binding recognition of the need for the "decolonization" of Palestine from its four-hundred-year rule by the Ottoman Empire and the reconstitution of the homeland of the Jewish people, its only extant indigenous inhabitants, in the Land of Israel.

In 1921, Britain reduced this territory by around three quarters to create Transjordan. That left the territory reserved for the Jewish homeland in 1922 consisting of what is now Israel, the "West Bank," and Gaza. That commitment, subsequently upheld by the UN Charter in perpetuity, has never been abrogated.[16]

The Jews are the only people who are entitled—through law and history—to what is now Israel, the "West Bank," and Gaza. The Palestinian Arabs, who have no such entitlement in law or history, want to conquer the Jewish homeland for themselves. *That* is colonialism. So, we should constantly refer to "Palestinian Arab colonialism and colonialists."

Zionism

Zionism, the movement for the self-determination of the Jewish people in their ancestral homeland, is the ultimate anti-colonial resistance movement. As a political cause, it developed in the nineteenth century to resist Ottoman colonialism; today it is in resistance to the Palestinian Arabs' attempt at colonialist conquest. So, we should refer whenever possible to "the Zionist anti-colonial resistance movement." If someone says in a hostile manner, "Are you a Zionist?" you might respond, "Yes, I'm part of the Zionist resistance to colonialism."

Jews

Jews are called Jews because they came from Judea. [17] So "Jew" is a perfectly good word to use. But the word "Jew" has its disadvantages. Over the centuries, it's been used in a disparaging way that reflects anti-Jewish prejudice: "To Jew" is defined in some dictionaries as to cheat or swindle. [18]

One option is to refer to the Jews as "the children of Israel." The term derives from the fact that the twelve sons of Jacob, who in the Bible was given the name "Israel" by God, headed the twelve tribes that became the Jewish nation. The phrase has the advantage of cementing in the non-Jewish mind the ancient association that is routinely denied between the land of Israel and the Jewish people.

Fight back against the weaponization of dishonest words against the Jewish people by weaponizing language that is true.

Believe in Yourself as a Jew

Too many diaspora Jews are apologetic about their Judaism because they have never been taught about its value to humanity and its centrality to the civilized and civilizing values of the West. They may think of it in terms of superficial cultural characteristics, like eating lox and bagels. They may flinch from its religious codes of behavior as being authoritarian, oppressive, and irrelevant to their everyday lives. In ignorance of the unique worth of those religious precepts at its core, they may believe that the secular ideologies to which they subscribe, on the assumption that they are moral, are synonymous with Jewish principles even though they are in fact inimical to Jewish teaching. As a result, they tragically subscribe to positions which, far from enabling them to fight back against the onslaught, actually form a key part of it.

In order to fight back, diaspora Jews need to understand Judaism, how this informs both Jewish and Israeli identity, and that it stands for the very best of good things, both for themselves and for the community. They need to learn to be proud of Israel and Judaism, not so that they can boast but to know that they are fighting the good fight.

Be Proud of Israel

To defend Israel's behavior in Gaza against the deafening accusations that it is a force for evil, its supporters need to understand that the IDF really is the most moral army in the world. That description is not hyperbole, PR spin, or exaggeration. It is true.

No other army goes to such lengths to avoid civilians being killed in war. Israel delivers leaflets warning of air strikes, it calls civilians on the phone to tell them to vacate their homes before it strikes them, it similarly delivers "knock on the roof" minor missile attacks to warn them, and it moved vast numbers of Gazan civilians out of harm's way in order to protect innocent life as far as it could.[19]

The result was that the ratio of civilians to combatants killed in Gaza, at around 1.5 civilians for every one terrorist, was vastly lower than has been achieved by any other army at war anywhere in the world—lower than the average of four or five civilians per combatant killed by the US-led coalition in Afghanistan and Iraq, and lower still than the global average of nine civilians for every one terrorist killed in war.[20] [21]

Contrary to the wall-to-wall claims propagated by the western media, the "vast majority" of the Gazan civilians killed in the war were not women and children. According to Hamas's own figures, there were some 71,000 civilian fatalities of whom around 51 percent were men.[22] Since Hamas's terrorist forces include even young teenagers whom they listed as children rather than men, the proportion of fighting-age males who were killed is accordingly higher still. Moreover, although children make up some 39 percent of Gaza's population they amounted to fewer than 21 percent of those who were killed.[23]

The IDF achieved this remarkable record in Gaza, moreover, in conditions of unprecedented difficulty caused by Hamas using their own civilians as cannon fodder, deliberately exposing them to attack so that the numbers killed would turn the West against Israel. Unfortunately, through the number of civilians who were unavoidably killed, and then through the Hamas propaganda that inflated the numbers and denied the truth that it was only ever terrorists who were deliberately targeted, the West bought into the big lie of IDF brutality. But Jews can be proud that the Israeli military behaves in a more moral, decent, and humane way than any other army in the world.

Be Proud of Judaism

Jews also need to appreciate the unique contribution that Judaism has made to the West's civilized values. While Christianity has obviously provided the West's religious scaffolding, Judaism is its foundation stone. Without it, Western civilization would never have turned into the intellectual, economic, political, and moral powerhouse that it became.

It was the principles of the Hebrew Bible that moved the West onward from the cruelties of ancient Rome and Greece to promote instead concepts such as justice, kindness, and respect for human life. These lie at the heart of the West's signature principles of humane, orderly, and civilized behavior.

The revolutionary Jewish principles of limited government and the rule of law founded in the consent of the people gave rise in eighteenth-century England to the core precepts of what would become representative democracy: the people were sovereign and one law ruled over them all. The framers of Britain's constitutional monarchy drew explicitly upon the principles laid down for the governance of ancient Israel that introduced the notion of civic equality instead of oppressive hierarchy and gave working people the equally revolutionary concept of a weekend day of rest from their labors.[24]

In America, the same kind of evangelical Christian founders drew upon the same Jewish concepts. As I wrote in my previous book, *The Builder's Stone: How Jews and Christians Built the West—and Why Only They Can Save It*, "The Liberty Bell that now sits in Independence Hall in Philadelphia is engraved with an inscription from Leviticus: 'Proclaim liberty throughout all the land unto all the inhabitants thereof.'… Benjamin Franklin and Thomas Jefferson chose for the Great Seal of America the image of the Israelites' flight from Egyptian bondage…. President Ronald Reagan's final address likened America to 'the shining city upon a hill,' quoting the words of the Hebrew prophet Micah—which had been repeated in 1630 by the Pilgrim Father John Winthrop, who imagined New England being as blessed as ancient Israel."[25]

Western science grew from the novel idea that the universe was rational, and that belief was given to us by the Book of Genesis, which set out the revolutionary proposition that the universe had a rational creator. Without such a purposeful intelligence behind it, the universe could not have been rational, and so there would have been no place for reason in the world because there would have been no truths or natural laws for reason to uncover.

The other vital factor for the development of Western science was the linear concept of time that was found in the Bible. This meant history was progressive, every event was significant, and experience could be built upon. Progress was made possible by learning more about the laws of the universe. All this is why many scientists from the earliest times onward have been Christians and Jews.

Jews tend to undersell themselves to themselves. They may talk up Israel's stellar humanitarian initiatives in rushing to the rescue for every plane crash, trapped caver, or natural disaster. They may celebrate the vastly disproportionate number of Jewish Nobel laureates and the enormous contribution Jews make to advances in medicine, agriculture, high tech, and so on that benefit humanity.

But they generally don't allow themselves to admire the indispensable role the Jews have played in creating Western civilization and the very best in social organization.

Maybe they're unaware of how central this role has been. But it also suggests an example of "diaspora neurosis." Centuries of being hated for being "the chosen people" has made too many Jews timid about even thinking there really *is* something special and marvelous about Judaism. Worse still, they may have themselves internalized some of the disdain that has come their way down through the ages.

This has to change. Fighting back involves above all self-belief. If they're going to survive, Jews themselves need to understand why it's worthwhile doing so.

Decide Which Opponents to Engage With

When deciding whether to engage with an opponent, you need to be selective. Some such people have minds that are hermetically sealed against an alternative point of view. If you decide to tackle them, be prepared to meet a brick wall and quite likely some aggressive behavior. Unless you are a masochist, or perhaps an exhibitionist who wants to make a scene, such individuals are probably best avoided in order not to waste your breath.

However, we are all having to deal with a culture in which more and more people, especially those under the age of about forty, no longer know how to think. They may well be highly educated, having had a university education. Nevertheless, thanks to the degradation of education over many decades through a combination of infantilization, social engineering, and propaganda, they too often combine profound ignorance and sheep-like conformism with a dogmatic belief that they are right.

For example, some of them are absolutely certain that Israel has been committing genocide in Gaza. The fact that the population there remained more or less stable in number during the war, that the majority of those who were killed were Hamas terrorists, and that if Israel had indeed been committing genocide, it would hardly have repeatedly moved the civilian population out of harm's way and allowed into Gaza millions of tons of food and other humanitarian supplies, makes not the slightest impression on such people.

Nor does it matter to them that genocide is defined as the intentional eradication of a people in whole or in part—which is clearly an entirely different matter from war, let alone a just war of defense, such as Israel's war in Gaza. Such people seem to think that genocide just means the killing of lots of people. They think killing people is nasty, genocide is nasty, and Israelis are nasty, so Israel must be guilty of genocide. It may be hard to believe that apparently intelligent, educated people can be quite so imbecilic, but that is the unfortunate reality.

So, they are the perfect useful idiots for the Palestinian Arabs, who for decades have projected their own intended crime of the extermination of Israel and murder of Jews onto their designated Israeli victims, turning criminal aggression into victimization and Israeli victimization into criminal aggression.

How do you tackle such a combination of ignorance, imbecility, and brainwashing, let alone malice? Even when Israel bashers aren't parroting the genocide nonsense, the disconnect from reality in their minds about the Middle East and their resistance to being corrected are intense and overwhelming, presenting a formidable obstacle to any meaningful exchanges.

It is possible, nevertheless, to make progress. It involves junking some otherwise automatic assumptions and developing tactics specifically geared to this most challenging situation.

Realistic Goals

Scale down your ambitions. If you think you're going to produce a lightbulb moment where a person who thinks that Israelis kill Palestinian babies as if they're stomping on ants suddenly exclaims, "I get it! The IDF are the most moral army in human history!" forget it. That's not going to happen.

Don't try to convert them. They are convinced that they know the facts because they're being told so by the media, the United Nations, the international courts, the big charities, and so on. In private conversation with such people, you'll sound like the tinfoil-hat brigade if you insist that these beliefs are all based on lies.

Instead, the tactic should be to change the conversation in a smart and focused way. Block off the accusation by a very brief refutation: "Actually, the majority of those killed in the war weren't women and children but fighting-age men." And then introduce what you want to talk about: "Did you see the pictures of the amazing meals being served in Gaza restaurants the day after the ceasefire? How do you think they got all that food so fast?"

We get overwhelmed very easily by the tidal wave of accusations against Israel and by the scale of the lies. Don't try to cover the ground. Restrict yourself to a few well-chosen words and then leave it. Keep it short, aim to open your opponent's mind by just a crack, and sow just a seed of doubt. This may sound like distinctly modest progress in recovering the ground, but it's better than leaving the soil totally scorched and barren—or yourself scorched or wilting.

CHAPTER 4

AMASS A VERBAL ARMORY

• • • •

By now, you may already be flinching at this. "It all sounds great," you might be thinking, "but how could I possibly respond so fast and so effectively? These accusations can come out of nowhere at any time. How would I even know what arguments to use, let alone produce them so quickly?"

The answer is that preparation is essential. You have to think tactically and be prepared well in advance. It's a good idea to assemble beforehand a few ripostes and one-liners appropriate for a variety of situations.

Here are a few suggestions for arming yourself against the barbs:

Barb: "You've stolen the land belonging to the Palestinian people."

Riposte: "Well, the Palestinians themselves say there's no such thing as the Palestinian people."

You can then quote senior Hamas official, Fathi Hamad, who said in 2012:

> Half of the Palestinians are Egyptians, and the other half are Saudis. Who are the Palestinians? We are Egyptians. We are Arabs. We are Muslims.[26]

Or you could quote Palestine Liberation Organization executive committee member Zahir Muhsein, who said in 1977:

> The Palestinian people does not exist. The creation of a Palestinian state is only a means for continuing our struggle against the state of Israel for our Arab unity. In reality today there is no difference between Jordanians, Palestinians, Syrians and Lebanese. Only for political and tactical reasons do we speak today about the existence of a Palestinian people, since Arab national interests demand that we posit the existence of a distinct "Palestinian people" to oppose Zionism.[27]

You could also add for good measure: "Oh—and did you know that Yasser Arafat, the terrorist leader of the Palestine Liberation Organization and the guy who invented the Palestine cause, was actually an Egyptian who was born and mainly grew up in Cairo?"[28]

Barb: "Free Palestine!"

Riposte: "Did you know the Arabs themselves have always said Palestine never existed and even blamed the Jews for inventing the name! In 1937, the Syrian leader, Auni Bey Abdul-Hadi, said:

'There is no such country as Palestine! "Palestine" is a term the Zionists invented! There is no Palestine in the Bible. Our country was for centuries part of Syria. "Palestine" is alien to us. It is the Zionists who introduced it.'"[29]

You could add: "Perhaps he said that because, before Israel was created, 'the Palestinians' was the term used to describe the Jews living there."

Barb: "If Israel didn't stand in the way of a Palestinian state there would be peace."

Riposte: "The Palestinian Arabs were offered their own state in 1936 by the British, in 1947 by the United Nations, and in 2000 by the US and Israel. In 2008, Israel offered them more than ninety percent of the "West Bank" for a state of their own. The Palestinian Arabs turned down every such offer of a state and instead redoubled their war of extermination against the Jewish homeland."[30]

Barb: "Israel is ethnically cleansing the Palestinians."

Riposte: "I do agree that ethnic cleansing is appalling. Did you know that Palestinian Authority President Mahmoud Abbas said in 2010: 'I will never allow a single Israeli to live among us on Palestinian land.' [31] So Palestine would be ethnically cleansed of Jews. Isn't that shocking?

"And did you know that, after 1948, eight hundred and fifty thousand Jews were ethnically cleansed from Arab countries—and went to live in Israel as refugees?"

Barb: "As a gay person, I absolutely support a state of Palestine to end Israeli oppression."

Riposte: "I wonder what sort of life you think gay people would have there? After all, in a sermon broadcast from Al Asqa mosque in 2022, an Islamic preacher said:

'Once Palestine is free, not a single homosexual will be allowed to live in our pure land. Such perverted abominations will not be accepted among us.[32]'

"Tel Aviv, on the other hand, is the most gay-friendly place in the Middle East. Where do you think you'd prefer to live?"

Barb: "Why do you misrepresent the Palestinians' liberation movement as being anti-Jew?"

Riposte: "In 2019, the Hamas official Fathi Hamad said:

There are Jews everywhere! We must attack every Jew on planet Earth! We will die while exploding and cutting the necks and legs of the Jews. We will lacerate them and tear them to pieces, Allah willing! [33]

"I think that's pretty anti-Jew, don't you?"

Barb: "Why do you support the killing of children in Gaza?"

Riposte: "Tragically, there are always civilian casualties in war, and my heart goes out to the children who've been killed in Gaza. But have you ever wondered why Hamas never constructed one single shelter for their civilian population? Not one shelter for their children and families, even though they built hundreds of miles of tunnels to hide themselves and to house the missiles and other weapons that they aimed at Israeli nursery schools and other Israeli civilian targets? Do you think Israel is to blame for that?"

Barb: "Israel has killed seventy thousand Palestinians in Gaza."

Riposte: "That's the figure from the Hamas-run health ministry that says it's the total death rate during the war. So amazingly, it means no one died of natural causes during that period! You've got to hand it to the Israelis. They've cured natural death!

"What's more, Hamas doesn't say that *any* of those people who were killed in all those bombing raids was a Hamas terrorist! Not one! So the Israeli Defense Forces must be the most incompetent army in the world!"

Barb: "Of course I supported Israel on October 7, but then they went too far killing too many people."

Riposte: "Hamas said it would repeat October 7-style attacks over and over again until Israel was destroyed. But in World War Two, around sixty thousand British civilians and around six hundred thousand German civilians were killed.[34] [35] Yes, the destruction in Gaza is horrible, and all civilian deaths are sad. But how many do you think it's appropriate for Israel to kill to prevent a second genocide of the Jews?"

Barb: "The Israelis have been committing genocide in Gaza."

Riposte: "The Israel Defense Forces literally phoned people in the path of their proposed missile attacks and gave them time to get out. Don't you think that's a bit weird for a genocide?"

Riposte: "The Israelis allowed into Gaza more than fourteen million tons of food during two years of war. Do you think the Israelis are the only people in the world to feed the people they intend to kill?"

Riposte: "At the United Nations World Conference Against Racism in Durban in 2001, a coalition of nongovernmental organizations approved a report declaring Israel guilty of genocide. Do you think this is the world's first genocide to last for twenty-four years? Or do you think that having been wiped out in 2001, the Gazans were somehow reincarnated so it could happen to them all over again?"

Barb: "Israel is a White colonialist country."

Riposte: "A majority of Israeli Jews are brown- or black-skinned because they come from Arab lands. Some twenty percent of Israelis are Israeli Arabs, who are brown-skinned. So, Israel is a predominantly dark-skinned country in which white-skinned people are very much in the minority."

Barb: "The Israelis are Nazis."

Riposte: "Mahmoud Abbas said his greatest role model is the grand mufti of Jerusalem, Haj Amin al-Husseini. He was Hitler's ally during the Holocaust, and he told Hitler that if he won the war, Haj Amin would exterminate every Jew in the Middle East.[36] So how come you're supporting real Nazis? I thought you were supposed to be anti-fascist?"

Barb: "The violent settlers attack Palestinian farmers all the time and destroy their olive trees."

Riposte: "Some of the behavior by Jewish residents in those areas is absolutely unacceptable. They should certainly be arrested and jailed. But they are mainly a few hundred delinquent teenagers out of hundreds of thousands of Jews living in these areas. And some of these incidents have been provoked by activists in order to film the confrontation and blacken the settlers' reputation. Did you know that the vast majority of violent attacks in these areas are committed by local Arabs *against* the Jewish residents?[37] Did you read about the pregnant 'settler' who was shot and murdered in her car when she was on her way to the hospital to give birth, and the baby died a few days later? Don't you think that's awful?"[38]

Barb: "Aren't we allowed to criticize Israel without being called an antisemite?"

Riposte: "Of course you can criticize Israel, just like you can criticize any other country. But Israel isn't being treated like any other country. Virtually every single accusation that's thrown at Israel is a lie or a distortion designed to paint it entirely falsely as an evil aggressor rather than a victim. No other country in the world is treated like this. And that's the point."

Barb: "Israel has killed tens of thousands of Gaza children."

Riposte: "The United Nations Population Fund reported[39] a rise of about fifty thousand births in Gaza from late 2023 to December 2024, when there were around five hundred and eighty thousand children under ten years old. In February 2025, the World Health Organization said it had vaccinated six hundred and three thousand Gazan children under ten.[40] Israel must be the first country in history to have increased the number of children it's supposed to have wiped out. Perhaps it has magic powers."

Barb: "Palestinian resistance is not terrorism but resistance to colonialism."

Riposte: "Zionism is the ultimate resistance movement against Arab colonialism."

Barb: "Israel is a pseudo-state because it was created by Western imperialism after World War One."

Riposte: "The same Western imperialism also created Jordan, Iraq, Syria, and Lebanon after World War One. So, are they illegitimate pseudo-states too?"

Barb: "Anti-Zionism isn't the same as antisemitism."

Riposte: "In theory they are different, but in practice they are not. Antisemitism has unique characteristics: accusing Jews falsely of crimes of which they are not only not guilty but are the victims, ascribing to them demonic power over world affairs, and viewing them obsessionally as a conspiracy to act in their own interests and put everyone else at risk. Exactly the same features that make the animus against Jewish people unique also characterize the animus against the Jewish state and make that unique too and in precisely the same way. Do you really think that's a coincidence?"

Barb: "Israel is like apartheid South Africa."

Riposte: "South African apartheid was an entire social system that deprived Black people of basic human and political rights and kept them apart from White people, even to the extent of having segregated street benches.

"In Israel, by contrast, Israeli Arabs, who constitute twenty percent of the population, have full civic and human rights. They mix with Israeli Jews, Christians, and others in parks and shopping malls, on beaches, and in swimming pools. They serve as Israeli police officers, judges, members of the Knesset, and soldiers in the Israeli Defense Forces. They study alongside Jews in the universities; they are treated alongside Jews in the hospitals.

"By the end of 2021, forty-three percent of new licenses for physicians were awarded to Arab and Druze doctors.[41] In January 2023, Dr. Abdulla Watad, thirty-five, a rheumatologist from the Israeli Arab village of Jatt, became the youngest Israeli physician to receive a full professorship in Tel Aviv University's Faculty of Medicine.[42]

"As for the Arabs who live in the disputed territories of the 'West Bank,' they don't have the rights and benefits enjoyed by Israeli Jews and Arabs because those living in the 'West Bank' don't live in Israel and so are not Israeli citizens. The suggestion that foreigners can be subjected to 'apartheid' is ridiculous. And the only reason they have to put up with queuing at roadblocks and other privations is because of the constant, active, and all too real daily threat they pose of murderous terrorist attacks within Israel.

"The accusation of Israeli 'apartheid' is so ignorant and misleading that frankly it amounts to apartheid denial."

Barb: "The Palestinians only want a state of their own."

Riposte: "In that case, why do they demand both a state of their own *and* the 'right of return,' which is the right to live in another country altogether, the State of Israel? Why should they all want the right to live in someone else's country unless they intend to take it over as their own?"

Barb: "I don't speak to Zionists."

Riposte: "Okay, but I'm identifying today as a Jew."

CHAPTER 5
EDUCATE YOURSELF

• • • •

Much of the helplessness felt by so many Jews when they come up against the anti-Israel onslaught is caused by the fact that they don't know enough to work out what to say. More troubling than that, their relative lack of knowledge makes them very vulnerable to the gaslighting being used to undermine them and leads them to believe that some of the lies they are hearing are true.

It's therefore absolutely vital to educate yourself about what's really going on in Israel and its dealings with its neighbors, and to educate yourself about Judaism, antisemitism, and the history of Israel.

Here are some common falsehoods and less commonly known facts about Israel and the Arabs that you need to know to combat the lies:

Falsehood: The Jews stole the Palestinians' land from them to create the State of Israel.

Fact: The Jews are the indigenous people of the land of Israel, the only people for whom it was ever their national kingdom and which existed for more than four hundred years, more than a millennium before Islam was created in the seventh century CE and the Arabs invaded.

Even after the Jews were conquered and exiled, they maintained a continuous presence there throughout the centuries of Roman, Arab, Christian, and Ottoman occupation, with Jewish majorities in several towns. From the mid-nineteenth century onward, there was a Jewish majority in Jerusalem. That was why, in 1922, an official British government policy document known as a White Paper said Jews were to be settled in their historic homeland—because it had been theirs. It said:

> It is essential that it [the Jewish community] should know that it is in Palestine as of right and not on sufferance. That is the reason why it is necessary that the existence of a Jewish National Home in Palestine should be internationally guaranteed, and that it should be formally recognized to rest upon ancient historic connection.

Falsehood: Israel was only created because people were sorry for the Jews after the Holocaust.

Fact: The UK first proposed a homeland for the Jews in the 1917 Balfour Declaration. The world powers followed suit in the 1922 Mandate for Palestine, which required Britain to settle the Jews throughout the holy land to reestablish their ancient national home there. Israel was created as a matter of historic and legal right which was agreed by world leaders some two decades before the Holocaust.

Falsehood: Israel is in illegal occupation of Palestinian land.

Fact: Under international law, those mandate terms have never been rescinded. As previously mentioned, the United Nations (UN) Charter says all agreements entered into by its predecessor, the League of Nations, remain in force unless they are abrogated by a sovereign state. That didn't happen to the terms of the British Mandate. So, although obviously the situation on the ground has changed, the Jews retain their unique legal, moral, and historical right to settle all that land—which consisted of what is now Israel, the "West Bank," and Gaza.

There is no occupied Palestinian territory because there never was *any* Palestinian territory after Israel was created. There was merely at the very least a legal no man's-land beyond the 1948 ceasefire lines, which marked the end of the Arab war to destroy the new State of Israel. The legal principle of *uti possidetis juris,* however, which holds that emerging states inherit their pre-independence administrative boundaries, means that Israel inherited the boundaries of the Mandate of Palestine as they existed in May, 1948 and so has always been legally entitled to all those disputed territories.[43]

Until 1967, the "West Bank" was indeed illegally occupied—by Jordan, one of the countries that tried and failed to destroy Israel in the Six-Day War.

UN Resolution 242, which was passed at the end of that war, entitles Israel to remain in control of these territories if the people there are still using it to mount attacks upon Israel—which is very much the case.

So the "illegally occupied Palestine" claim is ridiculous. Israel cannot be illegally occupying land to which it alone is entitled under intentional law, many times over.

Falsehood: There can be no peace without a Palestine state.

Fact: In 1921, Britain handed three quarters of Palestine to the Hashemite dynasty to become what is now Jordan.

That was, in effect, the original "two-state solution." Jordan is Palestine. The "two-state solution" therefore dates from before the State of Israel even came into being.

In 1922, the British undertook the legal obligation to settle the Jews throughout Palestine. In 1936, when both the British and the returning Jews found themselves targeted by sustained Arab terrorism, Britain offered the Arabs a slice of Palestine to create an Arab state alongside the Jewish homeland. The Arabs refused, as they have refused every subsequent offer of a state alongside Israel. While the Jews have accepted every such proposal for a two-state solution, the Arab response has been instead to wage yet more war or terrorism against the Jews.

The British offer to the Arabs in 1936 was, in effect, to reward them for their murder campaign by giving them part of the land to which the Jews alone were legally entitled, thus breaking the terms of the mandate. Obviously, if you offer an aggressor a reward for his aggression—and break your own treaty obligation to do so—you get not peace but more war.

By making this two-state offer, the British reneged on their mandate obligation to settle the Jews throughout Palestine in what is now the State of Israel, the disputed territories of the "West Bank," and Gaza. By tearing up international law, the British rewarded genocidal terror and set the pattern for a century of conflict.

Falsehood: The Palestinians are the indigenous people of the land.

Fact: There never was a Palestinian nation nor a Palestinian people. Judea, the land of the Jews, was only called Palestine by the conquering Romans who wanted to erase its Jewish identity.

No Arabs ever considered themselves to be Palestinians. In the 1920s, the Arabs living on that land at the time thought of themselves as part of an Arab nation. There was *no* distinctive culture, language, literature, history, or tradition based on the specific area known after the end of the Ottoman empire as Palestine. Many who lived there then weren't even Arabs at all. A 1920 British government handbook noted the following:

> The people west of the Jordan are not Arabs but only Arabic-speaking. The bulk of the population are *fellahin* [agricultural laborers of diverse backgrounds].... In the Gaza district they are mostly of Egyptian origin; elsewhere they are of the most mixed race. [44]

From the time the Jews of Judea were conquered and exiled, the non-Jews who inhabited "Palestine"—who we are constantly told were the ancestors of the Palestinian Arabs displaced in 1948 from their "historic" home—actually included not just Arabs but also Greeks, Syrians, Egyptians, Turks, Armenians, Italians, Persians, Kurds, Germans, Afghans, Circassians, Bosnians, Sudanese, Samaritans, Algerians, Tartars, Copts, Maronites, Ruthenians, Bohemians, Bulgarians, Georgians, and many others.[45]

Many of those who now claim Palestinian ancestry going back through the centuries are instead the descendants of those who poured into Mandatory Palestine in the 1920s and 1930s, many of them illegally, on the backs of the returning Jews who were seen as bringing work and prosperity with them.

There's an enormous difference between "people" and "a people." Palestinian peoplehood is a fiction that was cooked up in 1964 by the Palestine Liberation Organization's terrorist leader Yasser Arafat and the Soviet Union as a strategy to destroy Israel by claiming a spurious Palestinian national identity to bamboozle the ignorant West. It worked.

Falsehood: The Jews stole the land from the Palestinians.

Fact: Far from appropriating Arab property, the Jews bought most of the land from the Arabs—mainly absentee landlords. Many Arab sources have testified to this, including King Abdallah of Transjordan who wrote in his 1978 memoir that the Arabs were "as prodigal in selling their land as they are in useless wailing and weeping."[46]

Falsehood: Israel is a racist, "White privilege" country.

Fact: The majority of Israelis are dark-skinned. Some 20 percent of them are Israeli Arabs, Israeli citizens with equal rights to everyone else. In addition, more than half the Jewish population consists of Jews from the Middle East, the families of those who were ethnically cleansed from the Arab world after 1948. More than 850,000 Jews were driven out from countries such as Syria, Transjordan, Egypt, Lebanon, Yemen, Iran, Iraq, Algeria, Tunisia, and Morocco. Some of these Jewish communities had existed for more than 2,500 years before the creation of these modern Arab states. These are the majority of Israel's refugee population: dark-skinned Jewish refugees from Arab racial and religious hatred.

How Propaganda Works

In order to fight back, it's essential to get your head around the epic, near-unbelievable extent to which the public has been systematically lied to, manipulated, and duped.

Tuning into media discourse about Israel since the October 7 attacks—through newspaper articles, TV reporting, interviews, and panel discussions—has been to enter a parallel universe. It's been like following Alice through the looking glass into a world where reality has been reversed, everything has been presented through a prism of propaganda, and the grip on reality and moral sense of so many journalists has simply disintegrated.

Although this media mind twisting was unprecedented in its scale and intensity during the 2025 Gaza war, it merely repeated a pattern that had characterized the media for decades—and will continue long after the Gaza war itself fades from the headlines. Led by the BBC, the most authoritative and trusted media outlet in the world but which has grossly betrayed its own history, mainstream media outlets in Britain and America have consistently singled out Israel for malevolent treatment afforded to no other country, conflict, or cause.

It's not just that they get things wrong and exhibit gross ignorance about the issue on which they're reporting. Sadly, that's hardly unusual in the media. What's unique about their treatment of Israel is the way they have systematically reversed defense and aggression, failing to report terrorist or rocket attacks on Israeli citizens so that the Jewish state is falsely presented as the instigator of violence in the region, with its countermeasures consequently presented as aggression or "escalation."

Through loaded and hostile questions, the repeated use of terrorist-sympathizing interviewees, the total failure to report the genocidal and antisemitic nature of Palestinian society, and the reporting of Hamas propaganda falsehoods and blood libels against the Israel Defense Forces (IDF) as credible, the media has long painted Israel as oppressive, unjust, unfeeling, aggressive, and above all, in illegal occupation and in the wrong from the start by having appropriated another people's land. Every part of that is untrue. Reporting of the post-October 7 Gaza war ratcheted up this mendacious narrative to present Israel as positively demonic.

It's hard for people to grasp this total inversion of truth and reality because it really does seem utterly incredible. Many, if not most, who watch or listen to the BBC and Sky News in the UK, or CNN and MSNBC in the US, absorb much of what they see and hear as true. There's a powerful instinct to believe broadcasting giants, not least because people assume the video images they transmit cannot lie.

Understandable as this is, it fails to acknowledge how media presentations, particularly video or photo images, can all but erase the truth. Some of these images coming out of Gaza have been shown to be outright fakes, such as the pictures of skeletal children who were said to be victims of starvation but who were subsequently shown to be suffering from wasting or terminal diseases. Other distressing pictures or videos have been radically decontextualized, failing to show, for example, that the IDF were firing in defense at civilians who appeared to be advancing on them from the aid lines, or falsely implying that the children who were, in fact, sadly inadvertent casualties of war had been deliberately targeted by the Israelis.

Propaganda materials, particularly images, are crafted to play upon feelings and emotion because these simply drive out rationality and thus make factual evidence all but irrelevant. Even though pictures of "starving" Gaza babies may be faked, the over-powering emotions of pity and shock that they arouse imprint themselves ineradicably on the mind. Against the background of a media narrative claiming over and over again—but contrary to demonstrable facts—that the Israelis were callously and willfully killing children, the result was that these deeply upsetting images simply overpowered all evidence to the contrary that appealed to reason. And that insidious process has undermined belief in the rightness of Israel's cause among many Jews too.

Closely associated with this propaganda offensive is the tactic known as "gaslighting." Derived from the 1944 George Cukor movie, *Gaslight*, it means manipulating someone into doubting the validity of their perceptions, experiences, or understanding of events and believing instead the individual who is spinning a false narrative. It can make the innocent, or those defending the innocent, believe they're all guilty as charged. It can make defenders of Israel believe they have somehow lost the plot. And the Israel-demonization campaign has taken gaslighting of the Jewish community to hitherto unimaginable levels.

So, it's vital that you realize you are not going crazy, Israel is not behaving as it is painted, and you yourself are not to blame for supporting it. You need to realize every time you see a horrible claim about Israel's behavior that spoils your breakfast because it makes you so upset and confused that it's because the people producing such claims or images *intend* for you to feel like that. When you are shocked and distressed by a BBC or *New York Times* headline declaring that Israel has committed some atroc-ity, you need to understand that those words have been chosen so that, regardless of any true facts in the body of that very story let alone elsewhere, the headline's vicious smear about Israel is the impression you'll take away with you. You need to grasp that you're being manipulated and conned.

You need also to realize that, however indignant or bullish you may feel about such lies and abuse, a part of you may have been nevertheless undermined by it. The doubt aroused by this propaganda, and particularly by these harrowing images, is very hard to shake off. A small voice inside you may be saying, "Can all these accusations from all these people *really* be wrong?"

Several times during the Gaza war, I was approached by people who would say: "This demonization of Israel—the starvation lie, the genocide lie, the fact that so many believe these lies—is terrible, is ridiculous, is unbelievable, is a madness that's taken over. But…do you think there may be an element of truth in it…?"

The answer was always a very definitive, "No." If you look at the reliably ascertainable facts, at all the surrounding circumstances, at the body of evidence overall, and if you apply logic and reason to what you're being told, you will find that virtually every vile accusation against Israel turns out to be a lie.

It has almost always turned out that way. The scale of all this may be unprecedented, but the onslaught of lies about Israel is nothing new.

In April 2002, the media became hysterical over a Palestinian Arab claim that five hundred people had been "massacred" by the IDF in the "West Bank" city of Jenin. There were supposedly eyewitness accounts of Israeli bulldozers shoveling hundreds of Palestinian corpses into mass graves; stories of Israeli soldiers murdering Palestinian children in front of their parents and throwing their bodies into wells and sewage pits. In fact, only fifty-two mostly armed Palestinians were killed, as were twenty-three Israeli soldiers.[47]

In 2006, the Lebanese Prime Minister Fouad Siniora declared that Israel had perpetrated a "massacre" and killed forty people in the town of Houla. Later, he was forced to admit that only one person had died.[48]

And yes, images have repeatedly been shown to have lied. In 1982, during the First Lebanon war, *The Washington Post* published a picture of a seven-month-old baby that appeared to have lost both its arms. The United Press International caption said that the baby had been severely burned when an Israeli jet accidentally hit a Christian residential area. The photo so disgusted President Ronald Reagan that it contributed to his call for Israel to halt its attacks.[49] In fact, the baby hadn't lost its arms, and its burns were caused by a Palestine Liberation Organization attack on East Beirut.

On September 30, 2000, there was an exchange of fire between Palestinian Arabs and the IDF at the Netzarim junction in the "West Bank." The France 2 TV station released footage from the scene that showed a twelve-year-old Arab boy, Muhammad al-Durrah, cowering behind his father and then slumping over. The France 2 reporter promptly exclaimed that he had been shot dead.[50]

The image of the child cowering behind his father was broadcast around the world and directly incited countless Islamist terrorist murders of Americans and Jews. When Jewish American journalist Daniel Pearl was beheaded by al-Qaeda, a poster of this iconic image was displayed behind him,[51] as Pearl's father Judah subsequently recalled.[52]

But in 2008, unbroadcast footage of that event was requisitioned from France 2 by a French court hearing a libel action. When the footage was played, a packed courtroom saw the reportedly dead child peeping through his hand, moving his head, and without any visible bloodstains. I was in that court-room and wrote about it for *Standpoint*. This is an extract from what I wrote:

> The cameraman said the Israelis had fired con-tinuously for 45 minutes. Yet the footage did not show people falling under fire. It showed instead Palestinians demonstrating, throwing rocks and so forth, in a positively carnival atmo-sphere. Youths strutted about, giving declama-tory interviews and grinning at the camera; boys rode by on bicycles. And no one showed any sign of injury.
>
> There were no wounds; there was no blood. From time to time demonstrators were pushed onto stretchers and into ambulances—but with no evidence of any disturbance to their anatomy. The al Durrahs showed no sign of any wound or injury throughout. Supposedly riddled with bullets, their bodies remained totally unmarked. There was no blood anywhere.
>
> You see the boy slumping to the ground. But before he does so, while he is still hanging onto his father and screaming, a voice shouts in Arabic: "The boy is dead! The boy is dead!" Asked to explain this astounding prescience, [the reporter's] team replied that the Arabic actually meant "the boy is in danger of dying." At this the courtroom actually laughed out loud.

After [the reporter] pronounces the boy to be dead, the corpse mysteriously assumes four different positions. You see the cameraman's fingers making the "take two sign" to signal the repeat of a scene. And then you see the lifeless martyr raise his arm and peep through his fingers—presumably to check whether his thespian services are still required or whether he can now get up and go home.[53]

In Gaza, journalists have always had to toe the Hamas line on pain of being denied access, thrown out, or murdered. As CNN's Anderson Cooper reported in 2009:

Inside Gaza, press controlled by Hamas is heavy-handed. There are few press freedoms inside Gaza and Hamas controls who reports from there and where they can go. While pictures of wounded children being brought to hospitals are clearly encouraged, we rarely see images of Hamas fighters or their rockets being fired into Israel.[54]

In 2014, a former Associated Press reporter, Matti Friedman, blew the whistle on the total corruption of reporting from Gaza. He explained in *Tablet* magazine[55] how a deadly combination of obsessive prejudice against Israel in Western newsrooms and the tyrannical control by Hamas of media coverage meant that the Western public was denied the truth about Israel and the Palestinian Arabs, year in and year out. Routine threats to reporters or other stories about Hamas intimidation were shunted into the deep freeze. As Friedman wrote:

The policy was then, and remains, not to inform readers that the story is censored unless the censorship is Israeli.

The intimidation itself, however, was almost beside the point. Friedman continued:

> Most reporters in Gaza believe their job is to document violence directed by Israel at Palestinian civilians. That is the essence of the Israel story. In addition, reporters are under deadline and often at risk, and many don't speak the language and have only the most tenuous grip on what is going on. They are dependent on Palestinian colleagues and fixers who either fear Hamas, support Hamas, or both. Reporters don't need Hamas enforcers to shoo them away from facts that muddy the simple story they have been sent to tell.

Can everyone in the world be wrong about Israel while Israel itself is in the right? Yes.

It sounds incredible. It *is* incredible. But it's true.

This media demonization of Israel, in the service of those who want the Jewish state destroyed, can't begin to be fought unless people fully understand its extraordinary scope and impact—and how it is in turn merely the arm of a global liberal establishment that wants Israel and Zionism gone from its world.

How Do You Fight Against Media Lies?

Among those who recognize the lies the media tells about Israel, an understandable reaction is to write a furious letter to the offending outlet.

If the aim is to make the writer feel better by venting, fine. Whether it has any positive effect is another matter. It's not clear whether it does.

Media outlets certainly believe they need to know what the public thinks of them. Their profitability and continued existence depend on doing so. Personal correspondence to editors or comments on the outlet's website are therefore noticed and read. The BBC is so aware of the responsibility for fairness, balance, accuracy, and so on imposed upon it by its unique charter and public funding mechanism that it has a complaints department that publishes its findings.

During the Gaza war, several incidents involving accusations of gross BBC bias against Israel blew up into major controversies. Some of them, such as the BBC's use of the son of a Hamas official as an "impartial" narrator of a TV film about Gaza, left the BBC hideously embarrassed and forced into an apology.

In November 2025, an explosive memo surfaced that had been written by Michael Prescott, who until June 2025 was an independent advisor to the BBC's Editorial Guidelines and Standards Committee. This revealed that the flagship TV current affairs program *Panorama* had spliced together two clips from separate parts of President Trump's speech on January 6, 2021, and reversed the sequence of events to make it appear falsely that he had exhorted his supporters to go and fight on Capitol Hill. The BBC, wrote Prescott, had also repeatedly played down

Israeli victimization and Arab aggression to minimize Israeli suffering and paint Israel falsely as the aggressor.[56]

Yet none of these embarrassments has produced a perceptible change in the BBC's behavior. It continues to produce reporting that's grossly biased against Israel, host extremists and terrorist sympathizers as "impartial" studio guests, and pump out Hamas propaganda that demonizes Israel but is treated as credible. Individuals who send in complaints are routinely brushed off, which makes those complainants even more furious and frustrated.

So, is it worthwhile for an individual to make a complaint at all? In general, the smaller the media outlet, the more likely they are to take complaints seriously, because they can't afford to lose readers or viewers. However, it's also worthwhile—even with apparently impregnable megaliths like the BBC—simply because it's the right thing to do. To put it another way, if nobody made any complaints on the grounds that this would likely have no effect, these outlets would be able to tell themselves that their behavior was fine. If there's ever to be any chance that they may respond to pressure to change, the ground needs to be prepared by alerting them to the reality of public displeasure.

What is essential is that the complaint has to be temperate, never angry or insulting, and always backed by specific evidence of what was said or shown. Complain too often, and your messages will be junked as vexatious. Organized mass complaints are generally seen for what they are and are dismissed accordingly.

Choose your complaint carefully. Allegations of "bias" are far too vague and subjective to cut any ice at all. People who are upset by what they've seen or heard in the media reporting of Israel may also not realize that the point they're making, which seems so important to them, might be in fact a relatively arcane detail in the weeds of the issue. Limit your complaint to reporting that has made a significant departure from the standards of impartiality, fairness, or accuracy and that is incontrovertibly wrong, misleading, or unbalanced. Be prepared to produce the chapter and verse to prove what you are saying.

As in so many other areas of public life, journalists, editors, and media executives generally only sit up and take real notice of a complaint when it threatens their revenue or reputation among the people who matter to them. In America, this tends to be major financial donors; in Britain, it tends to be members of Parliament. These people, too, have reputations to guard, whether as custodians of the public interest or as investors in a product whose behavior might create a blowback on themselves. They will, therefore, be sensitive to the criticism of media malfeasance that, apart from causing them genuine personal outrage, might compromise their own reputation.

In alerting such people, there's a big role to be played by Jewish community leaders, which will be discussed later. Private individuals in Britain might ask their Member of Parliament to raise such concerns. The most effective avenue, however, is social media. Members of the public can post details of such media misreporting on X, Facebook, or other platforms and expose the lapses of individual journalists.

Such potential humiliation or embarrassment, being administered on what has become a universal noticeboard consulted by most people in public life, often has a galvanic effect. The public pillory function of social media not only creates potential ridicule or contempt for the journalist or media outlet whose reputation means everything to them but also alerts others to the ongoing scandal of systematic media disinformation. A post on

X can be far more effective than a complaint that gets swallowed up in the maw of a media outlet's complaints department.

Speaking of Social Media...

To counter the lies told by the mainstream media, it is essential to draw upon other sources of information. There's now a vast array of such alternative sources on social media and online that provide an invaluable antidote to the monocultural mainstream media's demonization of Israel. You can access websites, podcasts, YouTube videos, X, Instagram and other platforms that offer a wide range of viewpoints and information. Selecting some of these to access even once a week can act as a kind of vaccination to keep up your immunity against the poison being pumped out by the mainstream media.

But there's obviously a big downside to all this. There's a vast amount of vile and disgusting abuse on social media that it's prudent to avoid as much as possible. Moreover, precisely because such platforms have no editorial filter to act as a guarantee of quality, they constitute a kind of media Wild West where you can't tell who the good guys are and who the bad guys are amid all the shooting and the chaos.

Many people posting on these platforms claim to be journalists or experts but in fact have little idea what they are talking about and very often are incapable even of making the elementary distinction between facts and opinion. You can easily find yourself sucked down some really rabid rabbit holes of bigoted or barking-mad conspiracy theories. At the same time, sources that are neither bigoted nor crazy may still be unreliable and incorrect.

How to Know What to Believe

So how do you navigate these media perils and pitfalls? How can you work out whom or what to trust and believe in the midst of such a cacophony?

This is a problem that all of us encounter to some extent or another. The first thing to say may sound strange coming from someone who makes her living from journalism: Place complete trust in no one. Always retain an element of skepticism and an open mind toward everything you read, see, or hear. No one is infallible.

This may sound even more strange: Don't completely trust yourself. Be aware of what's called "confirmation bias," where you believe what you're reading or hearing because that confirms what you already think. That may be true of the sources you are drawing on, too. You may be attracted to sources that seem to chime with your own approach but that are nevertheless full of error and misinformation. And your sources may themselves be falling into precisely the same trap. Not everyone who appears to be on your side is reliable or correct.

Learn how to distinguish between sources that are generally reliable and those that should generally be avoided. How can you do that?

There are various tests you can apply. Avoid sources that are obviously banging an ideological drum—or access them only in the full knowledge that they are giving you a very partisan approach.

Be aware of the risk of a prior agenda behind the source. Be very careful about self-serving interviews in which a public figure is being allowed by an indulgent or even star-struck interviewer to promote him or herself. Alarm bells should ring if you don't hear the other side of a particular argument being given or if a controversial person fails to answer adequately any challenge about his or her known ideas or behavior but isn't called to account. Beware also of an interviewer who appears to be gratuitously aggressive or fawning.

Ask yourself if there appears to be a PR machine behind the person being interviewed. One clue is if he's popping up on your social media feed several times a day. Is he bombarding audiences? If so, this suggests you are being targeted by a strategy to promote him.

When it comes to the substance of the media accounts, there are other tests to use.

Is what's being said logical? Is it internally consistent, or are there gaps or contradictions? Does it make sense to you, or does it give rise to more questions in your mind? Test its propositions against other things you know that are relevant to the issue. Do they correspond with each other? Does any of this fit with what you know has already happened or what you think is likely to happen?

Tests like these are by no means infallible, but they can help you pick your way through the information minefield. And whenever possible, go to the original or primary source. If a newspaper story or blog post refers to an official report, a court ruling, or a statement from Parliament, the White House, or the State Department, look it up online. The story may itself provide a weblink; if not, Google some key words until you find it.

This may seem like a bit of a hassle, but it's worth it. Even the most reputable media sources may provide a story that misleads by selective quotation or omission, or else leaves out some crucial point that the reporter has failed to appreciate. On X or other such platforms, don't assume that videos are necessarily current or real or that quotes are accurate. Particularly with artificial intelligence, it's so easy to be duped. Check it all out as much as you can.

Recommended Sources

Here is a list of some sources that you may find useful in trying to gain a balanced and truthful picture of what's happening in the Middle East, Britain, and America. It's by no means a comprehensive list, nor are these sources infallible or uniform in their views. They all represent honest attempts by Jewish and Israeli commentators and other outlets to report and understand what's going on, even though they aren't all on the same political or ideological page.

Media Outlets

- *Tablet*: well-informed Jewish political and cultural magazine
- Jewish News Syndicate: straightforward, reliable reporting and opinion about Israel and America
- *Mosaic*: Perceptive American journal of Jewish ideas and cultural trends
- Jewish Virtual Library: comprehensive resource for information about the Jewish world past and present
- *Washington Free Beacon:* investigative journalism outlet, digs out facts and real scoops
- *The Australian*: balance and integrity in reporting and analysis
- *The Wall Street Journal* opinion pages: grounded in reality
- *The New York Post*: mid-market tabloid that regularly hits the bullseye

Organizations

- CAMERA, Committee for Accuracy in Middle East Reporting and Analysis: fights media bias against Israel
- HonestReporting: fights media bias, punchy, on point
- Israel Defense and Security Forum: online briefings by military and security officials committed to robust Israel defense
- Jerusalem Center for Security and Foreign Affairs: sound and authoritative security and foreign policy analysis
- UN Watch: nongovernmental organization that forensically exposes systemic UN betrayal of peace and justice in the Middle East
- NGO Monitor: research institute monitoring nongovernmental organizations that falsely claim to advance human rights and humanitarian agendas
- BICOM, British Israel Communications and Research Centre: news, analysis, and briefings on the Middle East; centrist
- Foundation for Defense of Democracies: well-informed foreign policy analysis; center-right

Podcasts

- *Israel Update* with Mike Doran and Gadi Taub: news and analysis about Israel and its relationship with America; center-right
- *Call Me Back with Dan Senor*: structural forces shaping Israel and the diaspora; centrist
- *Israel from the Inside with Daniel Gordis*: close analysis of Israeli society; center-left

- *The Ben Shapiro Show*: fast-talking, aggressive, incisive American conservative commentator
- *Ask Haviv Anything* with Haviv Rettig Gur: liberal Israeli commentator
- *TRIGGERnometry* with Konstantin Kisin and Francis Foster: open-eyed discussion with public figures

Commentators Worth Following

- Amit Segal: Israel's best-informed political commentator; @amit_segal
- Andrew Fox: ex-army major commenting on defense and the Middle East; @Mr_Andrew_Fox
- John Spencer: retired US Army officer and specialist in urban warfare; @SpencerGuard
- Richard Kemp: retired British army officer; military analyst, courageous public defender of Israel; @COLRICHARDKEMP
- Lee Smith: astute, well-informed American political commentator; @LeeSmithDC
- Liel Leibowitz: *Tablet* Editor-at-Large; Israel and America through a Jewish prism; @Liel
- Tony Badran: authoritative Levant analyst; @AcrossTheBay
- Michael Oren: astute former Israel ambassador to the US, historian; @DrMichaelOren
- Victor Davis Hanson: polymath, classics and military history; @VDHanson
- Kasra Aarabi: Authoritative expert on Iran; @KasraAarabi
- Salo Aizenberg: HonestReporting board member and indefatigable number-cruncher of false statistics; @Aizenberg55

- Eitan Fischberger: former IDF sergeant, open-source intelligence investigator; @EFischberger
- Mosab Hassan Yosef: Hamas leader's son who became Israeli intelligence asset; fearless fighter for Israel, invaluable insight; @MosabHasanYOSEF
- Khaled abu Toameh: Israeli Arab journalist, uniquely well-informed commentary on Palestinian Arab attitudes and behaviour; @KhaledAbuToameh
- Natasha Hausdorff: British lawyer; trenchant Israel advocate; essential truths about the legal case for Israel and the lawfare waged against it; @HausdorffMedia
- Douglas Murray: British journalist and author; eloquent and passionate defender of Israel; @DouglasKMurray
- Adam Kredo: US national security and foreign policy reporter, scoop-getter, *Washington Free Beacon*; @Kredo0
- Kimberley Strassel: *The Wall Street Journal*; shrewd American political and cultural commentator; @KimStrassel
- Oh–and me: @MelanieLatest, and melaniephillips.substack.com

Basic Primers on Israel and Jewish History

- *Myths and Facts* by Mitchell Bard
- *The War of Return* by Einat Wilf and Adi Schwartz
- *The Case for Israel* by Alan Dershowitz
- *A History of Israel: From the Rise of Zionism to Our Time* by Howard Sachar
- *History of the Jews* by Paul Johnson
- *Fabricating Israeli History*–The "New Historians" by Efraim Karsh

CHAPTER 6

HOW TO DEAL WITH PARTICULAR CHALLENGES

. . . .

Family and Friends

One of the most agonizing situations to have developed as a result of the campaign against Israel and the Jews has been that many family members and long-standing friends have become bitterly divided and even estranged from each other. Brothers and sisters, parents and children, husbands and wives have been horrified, aghast, and badly hurt to find that they have radically different reactions from each other to the onslaught against the Jewish world. Close friends from childhood are no longer speaking to each other. Adult siblings have broken off all contact.

Those who believe they are living through an existential nightmare—in which Israel is being defamed by lies that brook no challenge and in which the injustice and wickedness are as manifest as are the echoes of anti-Jewish persecutions through the ages—have been left distraught by the perception that some of those they love the most are echoing the defamatory lies about Israel. And, far worse, some of these are even blaming Israel for the Jew-hatred that they themselves are experiencing.

Of course, the people in the "Israel defamation" camp may also have hurt feelings, they may also be grieving at the rift with family and friends, and they may feel both pain and confusion at being accused by those closest to them who say, in effect, that they have sold out, damaged, and betrayed the Jewish people.

We'll call these people, to avoid confusion and for want of a better term, "conflicted Jews." Some of them may be openly anti-Zionist. Some may believe they are not anti-Israel, that they are only against "Netanyahu and his appalling far-right government." Some of them may have relatives or even homes in Israel, and they may think of themselves as Zionists. But all, to some extent or other, accuse Israel of behaving indefensibly.

We'll specifically consider the position of these "conflicted Jews" in a moment. For now, let's concentrate on the people they have hurt so badly.

What should you do if your nearest and dearest appear to have joined the ranks of the enemy as "conflicted Jews"? What do you do if you have a child who is so left wing that he says Kaddish for dead Hamas terrorists? Or if your wife believes Israel has been willfully killing Gazan babies? Or if your sister is so gripped by "Bibi derangement syndrome" that she thinks Netanyahu deliberately kept the war going, causing the deaths of numerous hostages and Israel Defense Force soldiers and horrifying Israeli voters, to serve his political ends?

Should you try to shock them out of what you consider their "self-hating Jew" attitude by giving them a piece of your mind? Should you remonstrate more equably with them and seek to persuade them with facts and logic? Or should you tell yourself that no cause is worth jeopardizing your ties with those you love?

Once again, there is no obvious or universal solution to this unfortunate situation. Much depends on the dynamics of the relationship—friends and acquaintances, parents and children, brothers and sisters. There's a hierarchy among these: acquaintances are clearly not as important as friends, and friends are in turn not as important as close family members. Or they shouldn't be. You need to decide case by case whether the damage you may do to your personal relationship outweighs your duty to set the record straight.

With those whose relationship with you is very close and very important, it's usually worth trying to put the case to them. Explain to them why their stance has upset you so much and what it all means to you. Listen carefully to the words they are using, and be sensitive to the feelings behind them, such as resentment, defensiveness, or even fear. Give them some credit in your own mind for wanting to promote the right thing, even if you think that it's absolutely the wrong thing. As with others whose viewpoint gives you grief, try to meet them at least a little bit of the way without giving ground on your own position.

Unfortunately, passions about Israel run very strong, and anger on all sides is hard to avoid. Minds tend to be closed if the position has been arrived at not through reason and evidence but through emotion or the grip of ideological dogma.

Ultimately, however, close family ties *must* take precedence over winning the argument. Nothing is worth destroying such vital relationships. But although the relationship must be protected, we must be true to ourselves as well.

The result may be a situation in which—and many are doing this—the loving relationship continues but with this issue never spoken about at all. This is far from satisfactory; indeed, it brings its own pain as the unspoken issue continuously hovers between you like a ghostly glass wall that seals you off from those you love. But it may nevertheless be the least bad alternative.

The Agonized "Progressive"

But what if you yourself are one of these "conflicted Jews"? What advice can you accept from this author, who is herself on the other side of this most agonizing of issues?

The views you have on this are of course your own, and this is not the place to have that argument out. But many on your "progressive" side of politics were dealt a bad blow on October 7, 2023, when a position you had treated as axiomatically right, good, and true suddenly turned to ashes in your mouth as 1,200 women, children, and men in Israel were murdered, raped, tortured, and burned alive by people you had long championed as being oppressed by the very people they had slaughtered.

That was devastating for you. And since then, you may well have been unable to process this. You've turned every which way to find a means of reconciling what happened on October 7 with everything you believe in. So, you may have denied that the Palestinian Arabs from Gaza raped the Israeli women. Or tortured and murdered the children in front of their parents. Or abused the hostages and desecrated their bodies when they dragged them into Gaza. Or you've said that if these things happened it was all Israel's fault because of its incompetence. Or because of its disastrously flawed strategy toward Hamas. Or because it had thwarted a Palestine state. Or because its government is so right wing. Or because everything bad in Israel is always Netanyahu's fault.

But none of these explanations sets your mind at rest—because none of them can explain what took place on October 7. So why can't you accept what actually did happen? Why can't you accept that Israel is victim rather than villain? Why can't you accept that Israelis normally tell the truth while the Palestinian Arabs normally tell lies?

The answer is that a powerful force is keeping your mind closed and causing you needless distress as a result. That force is the paralyzing terror of becoming "right wing." Its power lies in the belief common to left-wing people that everything that's not left-wing is both evil and right wing. And so, if you accept anything at all that goes against what you believe, including the evidence of your own eyes and ears, that must mean you are becoming "right wing." And that means you become evil too.

But guess what! That's simply untrue. It's possible to stop being left wing and still be a decent, good, and moral person. Indeed, it is *only* if you reject the lies that left wingers tell themselves and instead embrace reality and truth that you really will be able to be a decent, good, and moral person.

You may be worried that if you start acknowledging the truth about Israel you'll lose all your left-wing friends. Sadly, that may well turn out to be the case. And they may turn on you venomously for your apparent apostasy. That's undeniably painful. But it will certainly prove the point that they aren't good and moral people at all. They're actually vicious bullies. And you'll make new friends among the not-on-the-left people who aren't necessarily right wing or any wing at all. They're just decent and sane.

Trust me on this. I've been there, done that, got the T-shirt.

Professionals at Work

How should you respond at work if a valuable client, in the middle of advanced negotiations on a new contract, suddenly accuses you with no preliminaries of supporting "child killing in Gaza"? Do you declare you refuse to have anything to do with such a bigot and tear up the contract? Do you try to persuade the client that this view is twisted and the client has been conned? Or do you try to shut this line of conversation down as fast as possible?

As ever, it depends on the circumstances and on what outcome you're aiming at. Giving the client a piece of your mind may make you feel better, but it won't change the client's mind and may instead get you fired. If the client is of marginal value to your company—and if you're the boss—you may decide to take that nuclear option. If the client is important to your company, you may well decide prudence is the better part of valor.

Is it your duty, though, to hold this bigoted individual to account and clear Israel of this calumny? No, because this is not the right moment for a political discussion. Indeed, the client is out of order in trying to make it so and maybe was even hoping to provoke you into saying something intemperate. Departing like this from the agenda of the business deal is inappropriate and unprofessional and involves a confusion of roles. So it's not the right thing to do. Best instead to say: "I'd love to tell you the truth about this but I think this isn't the right moment for a political discussion. Shall we just get on with the task at hand?"

Students and Faculty on Campus

Students have long been on the front line against the anti-Israel and anti-Jewish madness and have borne the brunt of it—so have pro-Israel lecturers. The result has been a toxic atmosphere on campus in which Jewish students and pro-Israel academics are confronted by a wall of hatred, lies, and intimidation by masked and keffiyeh-wearing, chanting students who have sometimes made it impossible for them even to access the libraries. Lecturers and professors have faced intimidation, blacklisting, and boycotts. With some notable exceptions, university administrators have run for cover or tacitly supported the onslaught.

Whether you are a student or a faculty member, the overriding requirement must be to keep yourself physically safe. You also need to protect your state of mind so that, if you are a student, you can continue to study, and if you are unable to teach, you remain resilient and unbowed in order to fight back, garner allies, take legal action, and guard against depression and demoralization.

Safety resides in numbers. Whether you decide to fight or keep your head down, don't be alone. Join a Jewish society or similar group of like-minded people. That creates a vital sense of security and reinforcement that will enable you not just to express a frighteningly unpopular position when you feel you need to do so, but it will also protect you against the gaslighting that undermines what you know to be true. Student leaders and faculty should create safe spaces where Jews can remain proud Jews and support Israel.

In any public forum on campus, try to ensure that you are always in such a group. Actively seek out allies beyond the Jewish community. Whenever possible, obtain institutional support from advocacy groups and lawyers. Suppose you are being examined on your thesis about, say, Nelson Mandela, and the examiner asks why you didn't make a reference to Israeli "apartheid." Don't get angry and don't panic. Stay absolutely cool, avoid emotion at all costs, don't be disrespectful, and don't be aggressive. Act forensically. Draw the examiner's attention to documented sources to show that the analogy is inappropriate. If it looks as if this is going nowhere and you are being marked down, seek advice about tactics.

If there are lecturers teaching lies about Israel or promoting Islamist propaganda in their classes, start recording them, having taken advice from advocacy groups on how to do this safely and how to use such material most effectively. Send the recordings to the university administrator with a lawyer's letter. Set up a brain trust of academics to whom you can send the recordings and also send them to media outlets or post them on social media. University authorities that ignore such abuses because they are programmed to avoid trouble often react like scalded cats if they are faced with the prospect of damaging publicity.

Just Where Are Your Enemies Coming From?

There's a frightening range of people who appear to find it extremely difficult to have a rational conversation about Israel as their minds seem closed to evidence and logic. As ever, it's worth knowing what motivates them all in order to work out whether, despite initial impressions, some dent in their armor can nevertheless be made.

The Left-Wing Ideologue

Liberal universalists and ideologues to the left of them often seem implacably immune to any argument about Israel. They are so dogmatic that they seek to shut down all dissent by bad-mouthing their opponents rather than engaging with their arguments. Indeed, most of them refuse to engage at all with any individual who is making the contrary argument, confining their opinions to being screamed out in the streets.

Far from demonstrating how confident they are in their views, however, such behavior indicates the precise opposite. Left-wing ideologues are actually very vulnerable because they have an Achilles' heel.

As we have already seen, they believe that left-wing ideas are moral and decent because they profess things like compassion, fighting racism, and promoting the brotherhood of man.

But these left wingers are not driven, as they claim, by concern for the oppressed of the earth. They are driven principally by concern for their own reputation—to themselves no less than to others—as good, moral, and above all, intelligent people.

This narcissism makes them vulnerable. They are terrified that, if they lose the argument, they will lose in turn their moral identity and become—horrors!—"right wing" and thus evil. That provides an opportunity to expose them as hypocrites and charlatans at best and, at worst, as truly bad people.

They should be accused of being the thing they most hate. For example, academics should forensically expose colleagues who are peddling Palestinian propaganda as guilty of shoddy and useless scholarship, and their reputation as scholars should be shredded. People attacking the "Israeli settlers" for thwarting the establishment of a Palestinian state should be charged with promoting racist ethnic cleansing, since what they are saying is by definition that a Palestine state can have no Jews living in it.

The Israel haters have advanced their cause hugely by making Israel's defenders toxic. Having demonized Israel's supporters as defending the indefensible, they have succeeded in making anyone who supports those Israel defenders a pariah by association. They have correctly identified reputational damage as a priceless weapon in the war against Israel waged through the mind, and they have done so by using lies. Israel's supporters should turn the tables on them and use the same tactic of reputational damage as a boomerang against them, but do so by using truth and reason instead of lies and emotion.

Liberals with Moral Vertigo

Since October 7, another group of liberals has emerged. These liberals are not dogmatic but were so badly undermined by the slaughter of Israelis at the hands of the Palestinians whom they had so confidently supported that their minds were jolted open by at least a crack. This group has been conducting agonized discussions with like-minded souls—as well as with themselves—in which they are attempting to reconcile their views, which were held as an article of liberal faith in social progress, with what actually happened on October 7, at which they are peering in terror through their fingers. Terror, that is, of the potential collapse of their entire worldview, and therefore their identity, as they see it, as moral and good people.

It is possible to help such people continue this journey in the right direction. But it cannot be done by effectively beating them up for their liberal views—for example, by telling them that their belief in a two-state solution was always a lethal fantasy that has caused the killing of countless innocents. That kind of approach is extremely unlikely to encourage a willingness to listen. A more productive approach is merely to nudge them further down the road to realism.

For example, they may be unable to look at Israel's conduct of the war in Gaza without seeing the hate figures of Itamar Ben-Gvir and Bezalel Smotrich looming over everything as the people pulling Netanyahu's strings. The same people may believe that Netanyahu is the Machiavelli of the Middle East, whose every action since October 7 has been aimed solely at keeping himself in power. They may also think that Israel abuses the human rights of the Palestinians in the "West Bank" because the entire liberal priesthood tells them so.

There's no point telling them that Netanyahu is a great statesman, that Ben-Gvir and Smotrich are latter-day Maccabees, or that Israel is run by a supreme court that's obsessed with the human rights of the Palestinians.

It would be rather better to point out, for example, that if Netanyahu is indeed driven entirely by the need to keep himself in power, he's extremely unlikely to have deliberately kept such a traumatic war going for which the Israeli public would punish him severely over the loss of life involved, not to mention the murder of so many hostages. It's precisely because he's a consummate politician that he was much more likely to have been attempting to act in accordance with the Israeli public's demand that never again would they be exposed to an October 7 catastrophe or worse.

On Ben-Gvir and Smotrich, you might say that you agree that one or both are a menace, but they couldn't have been pulling Netanyahu's strings when they were outnumbered by his allies in the war cabinet. In addition, the power they are supposed to have wielded was always an illusion because they had everything to lose if they flounced out of the government, thus losing a status that they would probably never enjoy again. So rather than having Netanyahu over a barrel, it was more likely to have been the other way around.

And on the human rights of the Palestinians, rather than attempting to justify Israel's behavior, it would be more effective to point out that under the supposedly moderate Palestinian Authority—let alone Hamas—the Palestinian Arabs have never had any human rights at all but live under the rule of a tyrannical police state.

The underlying aim behind such an approach to liberals with moral vertigo is to encourage them to realize that Israel's situation and the people involved in it are all highly complex, that it's possible to hold several contradictory views about it all at the same time, and that therefore the highly polarized view they once had about it has no more connection to reality than a Tom and Jerry cartoon—and that they'll be better people if they realized all this.

The British Conservative

While most anti-Israel sentiment today is found on the left, it has a long provenance on the other side of politics both in Britain and America. In Britain, there is a strain of anti-Israel and anti-Jewish feeling among a particular type of conservative who is typically highly educated and often involved as an Arabist expert in foreign policy circles, whether in government, think tanks, or academia. Such conservatives view Israel and the Jews with high-handed disdain, and even contempt, and subscribe to many of the same falsehoods and distortions about Israel and the Arabs that are peddled by the left.

Such people will never change their view. However, if you do come up against them and are subjected to the elevated mendacity that is their hallmark and to which you feel a duty to respond, it's once again advisable not to defend Israel against the specific accusations they may be making—which are often intrinsically impossible to answer. It's far better to put them onto the back foot by leveling at them an accusation of your own.

So, you might respond by saying that Britain itself bears the primary responsibility for this whole Middle East impasse. It was Britain's foreign policy establishment that tore up international law in the 1930s when it reneged on its binding treaty commitment to settle the Jews throughout Palestine. Instead, it offered part of that territory to the Arabs in response to their murderous campaign against the Jews to prevent them from reestablishing their ancient homeland there. At the same time, Britain actually barred Jews who were desperate to escape Nazi Europe from entering Palestine, and so doomed them to perish in the Holocaust.

The British offer to the Arabs, which was repeated by the United Nations in 1947—and which the Arabs rejected in favor of all-out war to destroy Israel at its rebirth—was nothing less than another early "two-state solution." This actually represented a reward for murdering Jews and attempting to thwart the establishment of their rightful homeland. The British thus established the amoral pattern of rewarding Arab terror, by offering them land that's due under international law to the Jews alone, which has caused almost one hundred years of murderous Arab war to exterminate the Jewish national home. By maintaining this approach even now, Britain continues to punish the Israelis for the offense the British themselves committed against the Jews and the peace of the world.

All you need to say to such a supercilious British conservative is this: "People like you are responsible for the whole Middle East mess by having rewarded and incentivized the murder of thousands of innocents for almost a hundred years." He will almost certainly never have had that thrown at him before. He won't hear it from anywhere else.

The American Isolationist

In America, a troubling number of "Make America Great Again" (MAGA) conservatives are reproducing canards about Israel that reflect poisonous claims about alleged Jewish influence. These have a long history among American isolationists and were in evidence on the American right long before MAGA became a political force.

In their book, *The Israel Lobby and US Foreign Policy*, John Mearsheimer and Stephen Walt,[57] academics from the University of Chicago and Harvard's John F. Kennedy School of Government, dressed up the ancient canard of covert Jewish power to damage the world in the Jews' own interests as a legitimate scholarly analysis of Israeli influence over American foreign policy. Instead of being howled down as a piece of poisonous bigotry, the book became an admired bestseller, and Mearsheimer and Walt have been treated ever since as upholders of a principled American political position on the establishment right.

The theme common to MAGA and more traditional American conservatives is the fear that America will get sucked into foreign wars, in which such people don't believe that America has any interest at stake. Failing to grasp that the Islamists have declared war on America, they believe that the US is involved in the Middle East only because Israel wants America to fight its wars for it. They also believe that it was Israel and American Jews in the George W. Bush administration that dragged America into the war in Iraq. Some even believe that Israel was behind 9/11 in order to force America to fight for it. They find ways to blame all US foreign policy entanglements on the Jews.

Clearly, these are deranged conspiracy theories, and the people peddling them are profound antisemites. So there's no way that any engagement with them could ever change their belief that the Jews are behind everything bad that happens in America. It's nevertheless important to call them out in public, to warn people that such dangerous ideas have taken hold among influencers such as Tucker Carlson with his millions of followers. It's also necessary to tell people why these ideas are so worthless. Just calling them "crazy conspiracy theories" won't prevent even more people who are gullible from falling for them.

Jewish leaders and influencers should be pointing out to the public facts such as that, far from Israel pushing the US into war with Iraq, Israel told the Bush administration that it was Iran, not Iraq, that posed the real danger to America and the West. They should point out that the Islamic world has been at war with the US for decades, countless Americans have been killed as a result in terrorist attacks and in the wars in Iraq and Afghanistan, and Islamists regularly declare their intention to conquer America once Israel has been destroyed.

They should also point out that America's relationship with Israel is certainly not a one-way street of US largesse and Israeli dependency. Israeli intelligence is vital to keep Americans safe. US arms sales to Israel have produced hundreds of thousands of jobs for Americans to make those arms in America. And in Israel's October 7 war, while US involvement was decisive in taking out Iran's immediate nuclear threat, it was Israel that used its own air force and commandos to fight America's war for it against Iran, disabling Iranian air defenses so that US warplanes could attack Iran's nuclear installations in safety.

It's Israeli conscript soldiers, not American forces, who have been dying in the Middle East fighting against enemies who have declared war not just against Israel but against America too. Far from Israel sucking Americans into foreign wars, Israel is doing America's dirty work for it.

It's important that arguments like these against the MAGA and other isolationists should be made not just by liberals, who are in the isolationists' sights as promoting the globalism they believe is destroying America and who will, therefore, be dismissed as the "usual suspects" making these arguments. These points should be made by conservatives who cannot be accused of this, and whose stance in opposition to people from broadly their own side of politics will give these arguments far more weight.

Christians

Christians, particularly in America, are among the greatest and most passionate supporters of Israel in the world. However, liberal Protestant denominations, as well as the Catholic hierarchy in the Vatican, are among its most vicious detractors, whose hostility is inextricably bound up with theological Christian Jew-hatred going back to the early church fathers.

Many Christians are either ignorant of or seek to deny the terrible history of Christian persecution of the Jews, which caused centuries of punitive targeting, expulsion, and the murder of hundreds of thousands of Jews in Britain and Europe. Jewish community leaders need to call this out and hold the churches to account for the part they are playing today in the demonization of Israel; their failure to do so until now will be explored in the next chapter.

At an individual level, both Jews and Christian supporters of Israel should push back against this hostility by once again shifting the narrative. Rather than defend Israel against falsehoods about its behavior toward the Palestinian Arabs, they should talk about just who is protecting and who is ill-treating Christians in the Holy Land.

They should point out that Israel is the only state in the Middle East where Christians, along with all other faith groups, enjoy unqualified protection. The Christian community in Israel, of which about 80 percent are Arabs, has been steadily increasing in absolute numbers by 1 to 2 percent in recent decades.[58] By contrast, Christians have declined in number under Muslim Arab control in the "West Bank" and Gaza by 80 to 90 percent through religious and legal discrimination, desecration of holy sites, and social exclusion.[59]

In 1950, Bethlehem and the surrounding villages were 86 percent Christian. Since 1994, when the Palestinian Authority took control of the city, this has shrunk to 10 percent. As a report by the Jerusalem Center for Security and Foreign Affairs put it in December 2024, "Christian families are leaving Bethlehem due to systemic socio-economic hardships and instability, discrimination, and harassment (including of clergy) by Muslim Palestinians and the Islam-dominated Palestinian Authority."[60]

Muslims

How should Israel supporters react on an individual level to Muslims who express hostility to Israel in their presence?

Clearly, with Islamists orchestrating the global war of extermination against Israel, and with the Islamic world riddled by unhinged and obsessive hatred and fear of Judaism, encounters with Muslims are potentially especially fraught with tension and risk for individual Jews. On the assumption that such an encounter isn't physically dangerous, and that the Muslim individual seems reasonably open to a degree of engagement, the aim should be once again to reframe the narrative.

Try to avoid accusation and counteraccusation. Instead, undermine the fundamental assumption with which the Muslim person will have been indoctrinated: that the existence of Israel is incompatible with Islam. Ignore, for these purposes, the undeniable fact that Islamic religious sources are overwhelmingly hostile to the Jews. Make instead the surprising point that the Koran explicitly accepts the Jews' own special relationship with the Almighty and the Jewish claim to the land of Israel—and that a number of Islamic scholars have said so.

In verse 2:47, for example, the Koran singles out the "Bani Israel," the "Children of Israel," as having been "chosen above all nations" for specific blessings and responsibilities. There are numerous references to Allah assigning to the "Children of Israel" the land of Israel as residence (5:20–26) and as an eternal "inheritance" (7:136–137; 26:52–59).

Sheikh Dr. Muhammad Al-Husseini, a British imam who teaches a course on the Koran as part of interfaith studies at Leo Baeck College in London, has said:

> You will find very clearly that the traditional commentators from the eighth and ninth century onwards have uniformly interpreted the Koran to say explicitly that Eretz Yisrael has been given by God to the Jewish people as a perpetual covenant. There is no Islamic counterclaim to the Land anywhere in the traditional corpus of

commentary.... No fundamentalist, no matter
how hard they try, can overrule the existing tradition to say there is, in fact, an Islamic counter-
claim to Eretz Yisrael.[61]

As for the explosive issue of the Temple Mount, a nine-
page English-language tourist guide, entitled *A Brief Guide to
al-Haram al-Sharif,* published by the Supreme Muslim Council
in 1925, contradicts the repeated declarations by the Palestinian
Authority and other Islamists that there is no Jewish connection
to the Temple Mount, which they claim is Islam's holiest shrine.
The guide states[62] that the Temple Mount site "is one of the oldest in the world. Its sanctity dates from the earliest (perhaps
from pre-historic) times. Its identity with the site of Solomon's
Temple is beyond dispute. This, too, is the spot, according to
universal belief, on which 'David built there an altar unto the
Lord, and offered burnt offerings and peace offerings.'"

Make New Types of Alliances

One of the most unsettling aspects of the post-October 7
onslaught is that some people who were previously assumed to
have been the allies of the Jewish people have turned viciously
against us. Progressives who once identified themselves as standing with the Jews against fascism now demonize Israelis as fas-
cists and have turned their backs on the explosion of Jew-hatred
in the West.

Israel's supporters must seek to make new alliances. There
are plenty of people who would be happy to do so. Natural
allies include Hindus and Sikhs, whose cultures have never been

marred by hatred of Jews and whose communities have also suffered at the hands of Islam.

There are many potential allies in black and other churches. American Jews should park their long-held fears that even Israel-supporting Christians are all intent on converting them. Some are, many are not—and if they do believe the Jews will be converted at the end of days, we should surely take our chances on discovering the truth about their story when that happy event occurs.

Meanwhile, the Jewish resistance should actively court evangelical Christians to join forces in combating their common enemies in both the ideological secularist and fanatical Islamic worlds. Jews should actively and publicly campaign with Christians against the persecution and mass murder of Christians in Africa and other parts of the developing world where Islamic jihadists are so appallingly intent on wiping out Christianity altogether.

Interfaith

Interfaith work is worse than useless when it comes to fighting back against anti-Israel and anti-Jewish hate. Interfaith committees have long attracted controversy. Their supporters claim they build bridges between communities, break down ignorance of other faiths, and promote dialogue and understanding. Their detractors claim that, to prevent such encounters from falling apart, the most difficult points of disagreement between them need to be glossed over, and so the dialogue and connections are therefore necessarily superficial, leaving the core issues unresolved.

There's probably truth in both points of view, and so interfaith work will always involve unresolved tensions. However, it is a category error to imagine that, even with the good it may do, interfaith work can help fight the onslaught against the Jewish world.

Unlike members of the general public who might subscribe to such anti-Israel discourse purely out of ignorance, and who are therefore potentially receptive to truths of which they were previously unaware, interfaith work pits Jews against two religious ideologies, Islam and Christianity, that have a profound problem with Judaism at the very core of their dogma. Their hostility to Israel and the Jewish people, therefore, cannot be addressed within a structure that necessarily ducks divisive theological issues and makes no attempt to unravel the assumptions behind the dogma that is believed to be the ultimate truth by either Christianity or Islam.

It is as absurd to imagine that interfaith work can remove the sting of Christian or Islamic venom against Israel and Judaism as it would be to imagine that committees of well-meaning people could persuade members of the Chinese Communist Party to adopt representative democracy and human rights. Those rabbis who respond to the murderous incitement against Israel and the Jews by extending hands of friendship to the faith communities that are unapologetically perpetrating such incitement are helping to sanitize, excuse, and incentivize that onslaught. Instead of abasing themselves in this way, they need to fight back by calling out in unambiguous terms the religious rationale behind the campaign of demonization against the Jewish world.

Friendship can never be built upon a superstructure of hatred. Jews should not create illusory alliances with people who hate them. They need instead to cause such people to respect Judaism and the Jewish people and to hold them to account for their Jew-hatred.

Jews have habitually flinched from doing so. An innately peaceful and unaggressive people, they have understandably assumed that avoiding confrontation is the best way to guarantee their security and safety. This failed to acknowledge, however, the crucial fact that, beneath the interfaith radar, their Christian and Islamic foes were continuously confronting *them*—and getting a free pass for doing so.

Jews don't attempt to force others to agree with or adopt Jewish religious beliefs; they merely ask to be left alone to practice their own culture. For decades, Jews have pursued interfaith work in the belief that this was the best way to achieve that toleration. The baleful results of such appeasement are all around us.

CHAPTER 7

COMMUNITY RESPONSES

• • • •

Until now, this handbook has focused upon how individuals can fight back against anti-Israel and anti-Jewish hatred. There is, however, a severe limit to what individuals can do. An absolutely essential role needs to be played by Jewish diaspora community leaders. Only they are in a position to tackle the systemic forces that have driven public discourse about Israel and the Jews off the rails.

To play that role effectively, community leaders need to adopt a very different strategy. Indeed, they need to *have* a strategy in the first place. Astonishingly, they don't have one.

Certainly, there are individual community initiatives that have done excellent work in drawing attention to the egregious media bias against Israel, for example, or providing programs of assistance and advice to beleaguered Jewish students on campus.

These initiatives, however, have been scattergun. They haven't been part of a coherent and unified community strategy to take the fight to the enemy. Instead, the Jewish community has allowed the enemy to define and dominate the battleground. This has been catastrophically misguided.

Ever since the October 7 atrocities, Jewish community leaders have failed to rise to the challenge of what unfolded in the West. This has been, however, only the most conspicuous failure in a long pattern of communal inadequacy. For decades, these leaders have avoided speaking up plainly against the Big Lies about Israel and the Palestinian Arabs. These lies, which were left to metastasize throughout Western society, have been the fundamental drivers of the anti-Israel hostility in the West which roared out of control after October 7, 2023.

In Britain, Australia, and America, the Jewish community leadership—with some honorable exceptions—have conspicuously failed to say what needed to be said after those atrocities and during the war that followed. While they made occasional protests about specific and extreme anti-Israel malice, for example, the BBC uncritically broadcasting Hamas blood libels against Israel or the British, Australian, and Canadian governments recognizing a "state of Palestine" at the United Nations, they were mostly silent about the principal drivers of the madness.

They were silent about the virulent Jew-hatred that was the norm in British, Australian, and Canadian Muslim communities. They were silent about the genocidal agenda of the entire Palestinian cause. And they were silent about the fact that there was no "illegal Israeli occupation" in the disputed "West Bank" and that Israel's record in adhering to international law was second to none.

They were silent through a combination of timidity, ignorance, and left-wing attitudes that affected the way a significant number of these Jewish leaders themselves perceived Israel. With so many of them committed to a "two-state solution," they consistently failed to educate the world about the exterminatory aim of the entire Palestinian cause. With so many of them wrongly identifying with the British and American Muslim communities in the belief that these were being subjected to the same kind of bigotry against minorities that had afflicted diaspora Jews, they failed to identify and warn against epidemic Muslim antisemitism.

Above all, they didn't have what has given the Israelis the ability to defeat their enemies: the belief in themselves as part of a cherished Jewish nation, the homeland of a people that stretches back into antiquity and that forms the bedrock of their identity today.

For many, if not most, diaspora Jews, their Jewish identity is an add-on—undoubtedly a valued one, in most cases, but an add-on, nevertheless. They are British or American first, and Jewish second.

They don't behave as if their identity is under threat because they view that identity as British or American. They need to "fit in" to British or American society by downplaying Jewish nationhood. They are, therefore, on the back foot before they even start. Their posture is innately defensive, framed by their perception that their acceptance by British or American society is conditional upon "fitting in" to the mainstream.

It's undoubtedly the case that antisemites are very quick to claim that such a Jewish identity puts loyalty to Israel above loyalty to Britain, the US, or Australia. This charge of "dual loyalty," however, long preceded the creation of the State of Israel and was a signature antisemitic taunt against diaspora Jews stretching back into antiquity.

Moreover, it totally misses the point. Jewish identity is based on peoplehood, on membership of a culture defined by the ineradicable connection between the people and their faith in the land of Israel. The fact that this land is now once again the nation-state of the Jews does not mean that the loyalty of Jews who live in other countries is therefore innately suspect. There is no intrinsic conflict between their Jewish cultural identity and their national identity as Brits, Americans, or Australians.

Putting their Jewish identity first doesn't compromise or devalue the national identity of diaspora Jews any more than putting their family first—which everyone would presumably do—calls into question the loyalty to their country of every Brit, American, or Australian. Jewish peoplehood and Jewish identity are simply family values writ large.

Many diaspora Jews, however, don't just downplay their identification with Jewish peoplehood in order to go along with consensus opinion. More damaging still, many have absorbed into their own mindset the way their host society thinks about the Jews: that they are only a faith community and not an ancient nation, and so the nation-state of Israel is an impostor in the Middle East. Consequently, diaspora Jews find it almost impossible to demand that the Jewish state is treated in the same way as any other nation-state—entitled to be defined by defensible borders and do whatever it takes to ensure its security and survival.

As a result, when the West erupted against Israel after it was so savagely attacked on October 7, 2023, the Jews of the diaspora were left leaderless, exposed, and undefended against the onslaught. This has added immeasurably to their distress and confusion.

To fight back, diaspora leaders need to rethink their entire approach. No one wants to know about Jewish suffering. No one cares about antisemitism. The mere mention of it channels resentment and guilt over centuries of Western anti-Jewish feeling and persecution.

Antisemitism remained high even during World War Two and went underground only after the discovery of the Nazi extermination camps. The West will only ever show sympathy to Jews when they are safely dead and their fate can provide Westerners with the ability to be the heroes of their own story, like those who fought Nazism in World War Two.

So diaspora leaders need to stop trying to gain sympathy for Israel and the Jewish people. The aim today must be instead to outwit the propaganda that drives the threat against them, to undermine its perpetrators, and to use their own tactics against them whenever possible.

Community leaders need to stop groveling and start fighting back with a radically revised strategy. Supporters of Israel have always played defense. This means they argue on the ground defined by their enemies—"We're *feeding* the Gazans, not starving them! We're not committing genocide or war crimes; we're the *victims* of these!"—and therefore have lost the argument before they've even started. The accusation against Israel is intrinsically and utterly preposterous. Attempting to rebut it merely drags its Jewish victims into an alternative universe of unreason, baseless hatred, and moral bankruptcy.

There's a need to go from the back foot onto the front foot, from playing defense to offense. This means not waiting for attacks to which to respond but taking the initiative by attacking opponents and doing so on their own ground where their vulnerabilities lie.

How to Fight Back

Here's what community leaders need to be doing if they are to lead a fight back against the hate:

- Tell the Western public directly how their media and governments are lying to them about Israel. Invest as a matter of urgency in a properly staffed, financed, and directed daily media rebuttal strategy. Publicly name and shame media outlets and individual journalists that publish lies and disruptions about Israel. Provide a daily bulletin detailing the falsehoods and distortions of the BBC and Sky News, *The New York Times* and *The Guardian*, CNN and MSNBC, as well as the baleful influence on all these outlets of the venomously post-Zionist Israeli newspaper, *Haaretz,* upon whose English edition so many Western media outlets draw. Post these materials on social media.

- Combat the lies by telling the public some basic truths about Israel and the Arabs that community leaders have always flinched from doing, because they don't know them, are too frightened to speak to them, or have an ideological problem with acknowledging them.

- Address head-on the basic lie of "Palestine." Start telling the Western public what the vast majority have never been taught: the history of Palestine under the mandate that created it as a homeland for the Jews; how most of today's "Palestinians" descend from those who immigrated from neighboring states to benefit from the Jews' return to the land; and how the British tore up international law and rewarded Arab terrorism by offering them part of the Jews' homeland and allowing illegal Arab immigration, while excluding the Jews trying to flee Nazi persecution.

- Junk the false distinction made for decades between ordinary Palestinian Arabs and their terrorist leaders, and make public the copious evidence—from their own words, from their flags and insignia, from opinion polling, from what they teach their children and from their actions in heroizing and rewarding terrorists—that the Palestinian Arabs overwhelmingly want to destroy Israel and murder Jews. Publicize the historical evidence that "Palestinianism" is a fiction created in the 1960s with the sole purpose of exterminating Israel and is built entirely on stealing from the Jews not just their homeland but their ancient history in the land.

- Draw public attention to the alliance between the Arabs of Mandatory Palestine and Hitler, the post-war settlement of Nazis in the Arab world, and the unbroken links between today's "Palestinian" leadership and Nazi ideology, highlighting every statement by the Palestinian Authority that regularly draws upon Nazi-style demonization of the Jews.

- Show that there never was a Palestinian people and that there is no legal, historical, or moral Palestinian claim to the land. Provide the legal and historical proof that the claim of "illegal Jewish settlements" in the disputed "West Bank" territories is a lie and that the Jews are the *only* people with a legal and historic claim to the land.

- Rebut the false claim of Palestinian entitlement to the land by showing that the Jews are the indigenous people of Israel, which has only ever been the national kingdom of the Jews alone. Publicize the copious evidence that the Palestinian cause is merely a disguise for the Islamic religious war that's been waged for the last century against the Jewish homeland. Draw upon the astonishing heroism and love of nation displayed by the Jewish, Druze,

Muslim, and other Israel Defense Forces soldiers during the October 7 war to embody in multiethnic form the inspirational ethos of those who defended the ancient kingdom of Israel three thousand years ago.

- Stop focusing on dead Jews by obsessing over Holocaust memorialization and start concentrating instead on admiration for live ones.

- Promote a love of Judaism and Israel within the Jewish community.

- Counter the anti-Israel propaganda in schools by developing curricula that teach the truth about the Jews and their history in the land of Israel.

- Inspire Jewish schoolchildren by teaching them the virtues of Jewish principles, as well as the self-destructiveness of universalist Western ideas and the harm these have done to Israel. Develop structures to challenge the suicidal ideologies of the left that have captured not only the universities, media, and cultural classes but also much of the security establishment.

- Create and fund structures that can deliver a comprehensive strategy to strengthen resilience in the Jewish community. Teach young Jews to be proud of Israel. Counter the lies to which they are exposed about "occupation," "illegality," and "disproportionate killing," and give them the evidence that shows these are falsehoods. Plug the gaping holes in Jewish education that teaches religiously observant form over substance. Teach the history of the Jews in the land of Israel and the greatness of the moral principles of Judaism. Show young people the key role Judaism has played in creating the core values of Western civilization.

- Counter anti-Zionism and demonstrate, by teaching that Judaism consists of the unbreakable bond between the people, the religion, and the land, that anti-Zionism seeks to destroy the essence of Judaism itself.

- Deploy weapons of persuasion based on truth against those who have used such tactics to demonize Israel and the Jews with lies. Expose their manipulative methods in forensic fashion and detail the alliances between them that have undermined not just Israel but the West. Track their anti-Israel, anti-Western, or Islamist funding streams, and expose their influence over the global humanitarian establishment—from the big nongovernmental organizations and international courts to the United Nations and its satellite bodies—that is bent on delegitimizing and destroying Israel.

- Set factions in the anti-Israel alliance—Islamists, leftists, feminists, "Queers for Palestine"—against each other. Name and shame specific individuals, institutions, and groups, exposing their ignorance and malice and thus holding them up to clearly deserved public ridicule and contempt. Show the public how these groups have manipulated them and played them for suckers.

- Recognize that the onslaught against the Jews is a phenomenon that repudiates reason. Therefore, approach this as if fighting a cult, drawing upon the experience of those who have deprogrammed cult members. Develop tactics to counter the strategy of "psyops"—or psychological warfare—that was taught to the Islamist world by the Soviet Union and that the Islamists have used to such significant effect in this onslaught.

- Target the progressives' Achilles' heel—their overwhelming concern to maintain their reputation as moral and virtuous. Flip the script and show how, in fact, they embody the very things they purport to hate.

- Reclaim the language to restore the proper meaning of words, such as "justice," "racism," and "genocide," that have been hijacked to twist the Western mind into believing that things are the opposite of what they really are.

- Harness the cause of Israel and the Jews to the wider and related cause of defending Western civilization. Create a resistance movement that brings together like-minded people from all walks of life to run campaigns involving educational programs, publications, videos, podcasts, symposia, and other public events.

- Use the mechanisms of civil society—the courts, grant-funding bodies, and grassroots campaign movements that empower the silent majority—to take back control of institutions and professions that have been hijacked by left-wing ideologues hostile to both Israel and Western civilization. Hold large-scale events with speakers who will pull in the crowds and attract media attention.

- Provide legal help for those who have been victimized because of their beliefs or ideas so they can take their oppressors—and those who enable them, such as university authorities—to court. Mobilize an army of keyboard warriors to deploy shrewdly crafted, evidence-based truth bombs against the lies and conspiracy theories that pollute social media and incite hatred and worse.

- Form alliances to take on Islamization. Join parents, teachers, political activists, and others to expose Islamists trying to influence what is taught in schools or infiltrating political parties, local councils, and charities.

- Create alliances to fight left-wing ideologies involved in the demonization of Britain, the Western nation-state, and the biblical roots of the West. Name and shame the media, universities, and churches for betraying their own core principles of objectivity, scholarship, and truth in demonizing Israel and facilitating Jew-hatred. Use lawsuits to hold accountable those spreading hate and incitement and their administrators who are turning a blind eye. Demand that all levers of the state are used to ensure that public money is not used to promote such demonization and incitement.

- Drive a wedge between the cultural elites and the general public by identifying the growing Islamization of the West and elite spinelessness in response. Demand that the Muslim Brotherhood be proscribed in both Britain and America. Form a cross-cultural alliance to fight the deployment of "Islamophobia" to silence criticism of the Islamic world.

- Call out Muslim antisemitism as a community-wide issue. Name and shame political parties that connive with Islamist forces committed to the destruction of Israel and the conquest of the West. Call out the churches over abandoning Christians persecuted by Islamists while reverting to the ancient Christian calumny of replacement theology, which casts the Jews as demonic for denying the divinity of Jesus, and which has been revived under the stimulus of support for Palestinianism.

- Call out also those Jews and Jewish groups who help spread libelous falsehoods about Israel. Israel's defenders flinch from doing so because the Jewish world tells itself that the greatest threat it faces is disunity, which has brought disaster upon the Jewish people in the past because it has fatally weakened its defense against its enemies.

How to Stop Sabotaging the Fight Back

While it is undeniable that disunity is disastrous, an even greater catastrophe is threatened by Jews turning against their own. This provides both lethal weaponry and a protective shield for the mortal enemies of the Jewish people. These anti-Jewish Jews have joined forces with those who are intent upon the extermination of the Jewish state.

There is, however, another reason why these anti-Jewish Jews aren't held accountable by the Jewish community, and that's its extreme reluctance to see left-wing ideologues as a threat. This is particularly true of American Jews, some three-quarters of whom are on the liberal or left wing of both politics and religion. They retain a fixed belief that the principal threat to the Jews comes from the extreme right, despite the fact that most of this threat emanates from progressives and the radicals of race, gender, and climate politics. And that perverse belief derives in large measure from the fact that these radical ideologies are endorsed by liberal Jews themselves.

They do so to ingratiate themselves with people they value, such as university academics, media, and other cultural elites who claim that peace and justice depend on giving the Palestinians their "rights." They also do so because their ignorance of Judaism means they don't understand that the ideologies they have embraced are a dagger at its heart.

Rather than fight those who victimize Jews for defending themselves against attack, they join the herd in blaming Jews for their own victimization.

The damage that's been done by Jews who have a pathological impulse to damage their own people, and who hurl against Israel and Zionism the same malevolent lies deployed by those who want Israel and the Jews removed from the world, is unconscionable. The willful refusal by the Jewish community leadership to address this amounts to a betrayal of a Jewish community that's under siege.

Fighting back against the onslaught demands that the community's leaders now step up to the plate and denounce such Jews as pariahs and beyond the pale as traitors to their people. But that demands in turn that these leaders understand what it means to be a proud and committed Jew.

In order to fight back, they first need to educate themselves about Jewish identity and understand the lesson that Israel has been teaching the diaspora and the West ever since October 7, 2023—that in order to have a future, a people must connect its present to its past.

Israel fights its mortal foes so effectively because it knows and loves what it is—a nation whose identity is formed by its history in the land founded on its ancient faith. Besieged by a society that disdains all such distinctiveness, diaspora Jews must slough off the West's seductive but fatal embrace and identify instead with their ancient nation.

That's the essential first step. Everything else follows from that. Only then can the Jewish people properly fight back.

CHAPTER 8
THUMBNAIL PRINCIPLES FOR FIGHTING BACK

- Stand up for yourself as a proud Jew. Equip yourself with arguments and strategies to deal with unpleasant or upsetting prejudice.
- Keep calm and evidence-based at all times and never give way to anger and insult.
- Guard against demoralization and excessive sadness.
- Don't take risks with your safety. Learn to distinguish between cowardice and recklessness.
- Educate yourself about what's really going on in Israel and its dealings with its neighbors and about Judaism, antisemitism, and the history of Israel.
- Get smart rather than emotional.
- Understand your opponents.
- Equip yourself in advance with a verbal armory.

- Cultivate like-minded friends and make alliances with people who will always have your back.
- Move from playing defense to going on the offense.
- Reframe the narrative.
- Shift the argument onto the ground of your own choosing.
- Use weapons of psychological warfare and reputational damage against your tormentors.
- Address head-on the lies about Israel and "Palestine."
- Reclaim the language to restore the proper meaning of words that have been hijacked.
- Be positive about Israel.
- Ditch the obsession with Holocaust memorialization. Focus instead on live Jews.
- Call out Muslim antisemitism.
- Call out the Jewish Israel haters.
- Create a resistance movement to take back control of institutions that have been hijacked by anti-Western ideologies.
- Develop curricula to counter anti-Israel propaganda in schools.
- Teach Jewish children to love Judaism, Israel, and the Jewish people.
- Believe in the greatness of the eternal Jewish people.
- Keep authentic Jewish principles—as well as an open mind and a suitcase packed.

CONCLUSION

For diaspora Jews, the shock of this onslaught, in addition to the trauma of the October 7 atrocities in Israel, is immeasurable. The feeling of somehow stepping into an alternative universe is all but paralyzing. The scale of the current challenge to living a normal, tranquil, secure life—the life that diaspora Jews thought they had previously been living—seems insurmountable.

We don't know how this situation will develop. There are too many known unknowns and unknown unknowns. Diaspora Jews may decide in increasing numbers that they have no future unless they move to Israel.

Many will not do that. And much can indeed be done to fight back if equipped with the right attitude.

That means casting off the diaspora mentality of cultural cringe—keeping heads below the parapet, seeking to efface Jewish distinctiveness, always fearful of adverse reactions by the host society. Instead, Jews in Western society should rediscover the ancient Jewish fighting spirit that animated the heroes of ancient Israel in their battles against enemies who sought their annihilation from the world. As they do today.

It's the historic duty of the Jewish people to bear witness to what is taking place in the world. It's also our duty to our children and grandchildren to fight for truth and justice. For this is not just about fighting murderous hatred. It's also about reconnecting Jews to what they most fundamentally are. It's about the most crucial factor behind the astonishing survival of the Jews throughout the centuries: Jewish continuity.

It's about rediscovering, renewing, and reasserting the greatness of the Jewish people—the treatment of whom will determine whether Western culture survives or disintegrates in the seismic battle now under way between civilization and barbarism. It's a choice that all of us must make.

ENDNOTES

• • • •

1   "AJC Survey Shows American Jews Are Deeply and Increasingly
    Connected to Israel," AJC, effective June 10, 2024, https://www.ajc.
    org/news/ajc-survey-shows-american-jews-are-deeply-and-
    increasingly-connected-to-israel.

2   Eleanor Mann and Ian Leonard, "NHS Doctor Who Praised Hamas
    Attacks and Arrived at Tribunal Hearing Wearing 'Celebratory'
    October 7 Necklace Is Suspended for 15 Months," *Daily Mail*,
    November 26, 2025, https://www.dailymail.co.uk/news/article-
    15329357/NHS-doctor-praised-Hamas-attacks-arrived-tribunal-
    hearing-wearing-celebratory-October-7-necklace-suspended-15-
    months.html.

3   JN Reporter, "CAA to Bring Court Challenge After 'Jewish
    Supremacy' Doctor Allowed to Keep Licence," *Jewish News*, October
    7, 2025, https://www.jewishnews.co.uk/caa-to-bring-court-challenge-
    after-jewish-supremacy-doctor-allowed-to-keep-licence/.

4   John Spencer, "Israel Implemented More Measures to Prevent
    Civilian Casualties Than Any Other Nation in History | Opinion,"
    Newsweek, January 31, 2024, https://www.newsweek.com/
    israel-implemented-more-measures-prevent-civilian-casualties-any-
    other-nation-history-opinion-1865613.

5   IDF Editorial Team, "How Is the IDF Minimizing Harm to
    Civilians in Gaza?" Israel Defense Forces, effective July 16, 2014,

https://www.idf.il/en/mini-sites/hamas/how-is-the-idf-minimizing-harm-to-civilians-in-gaza/.

6   AP Reporters, "Israel Tells Gaza City Residents to Move to Safe Zone as It Expands Operations," *Nation.Cymru*, September 6, 2025, https://nation.cymru/news/israel-tells-gaza-city-residents-to-move-to-safe-zone-as-it-expands-operations/.

7   Jewishnews_au, "As missiles rained down, an Israeli Arab Muslim woman found shelter in a synagogue," Instagram, June 19, 2025, https://www.instagram.com/reel/DLEvQ6BO2o0/.

8   Mouna Maroun, "I'm an Israeli Arab. I'm Embarrassed—and Hamas Is to Blame | Opinion," *Newsweek*, November 21, 2023, https://www.newsweek.com/im-israeli-arab-hamas-does-not-represent-me-opinion-1845763.

9   The "West Bank" is in quote marks because it is a contested rather than a politically neutral term. It is properly merely a geographical description of the area on the west bank of the Jordan River. However, it is used as a proper noun designating a territory to erase the fact that it is the ancient Jewish land of Judea and Samaria.

10   Home Page, I'm That Jew, accessed January 12, 2026, https://imthatjew.com/.

11   Joshua Teitelbaum and Lt. Col. (ret.) Michael Segall, "The Iranian Leadership's Continuing Declarations of Intent to Destroy Israel," Jerusalem Center for Public Affairs, 2012, https://jcpa.org/wp-content/uploads/2012/05/IransIntent2012b.pdf.

12   Joshua Teitelbaum, "The Iranian Leadership's Continuing Declarations of Intent to Destroy Israel," 2012, https://jcpa.org/wp-content/uploads/2012/05/IransIntent2012b.pdf.

13   Yair Rosenberg, "Did Netanyahu Put Anti-Semitic Words in Hezbollah's Mouth?" *Tablet*, March 9, 2015, https://www.tabletmag.com/sections/news/articles/did-netanyahu-put-anti-semitic-words-in-hezbollahs-mouth.

14   Jerusalem Post Staff, "'A Fatwa for Genocide' – Wiesenthal Center Slams Hamas Charter," *The Jerusalem Post*, July 14, 2019, https://www.jpost.com/Israel-News/A-Fatwa-for-Genocide-Wiesenthal-center-slams-Hamas-charter-595634.

15 Pinhas Inbari, "Will Fatah Give Up the Armed Struggle at Its Sixth General Congress?" *Jerusalem Issue Briefs* 9, no. 6 (2009), https://aijac.org.au/update/fatah-s-general-conference/#Article_3.

16 Robert L. Meyer, "Israel Under Fire – The Attempt to Deny the Foundational Legal, Historical, and National Rights of the Jewish People," Jerusalem Center for Security and Foreign Affairs, accessed January 12, 2026, https://jcpa.org/article/the-attempt-to-deny-the-foundational-legal-historical-and-national-rights-of-the-jewish-people/.

17 Britannica Editors, "Judaea," *Britannica*, accessed January 12, 2026, https://www.britannica.com/place/Judaea.

18 "Jew," Oxford English Dictionary, accessed January 12, 2026, https://www.oed.com/dictionary/jew_v .

19 Jack Elbaum, "West Point Urban Warfare Expert: IDF 'Implemented More Measures to Prevent Civilian Casualties Than Any Other Military in History'," *The Algemeiner*, February 1 2024, https://www.algemeiner.com/2024/02/01/west-point-urban-warfare-expert-idf-implemented-more-measures-to-prevent-civilian-casualties-than-any-other-military-in-history/.

20 Aizenberg (@Aizenberg55), "Gaza Fatality Analysis: Latest Findings from Hamas & IDF Data," Twitter (now X), September 29, 2025, https://x.com/Aizenberg55/status/1972667839409504518.

21 "Ninety Per Cent of War-Time Casualties Are Civilians, Speakers Stress, Pressing Security Council to Fulfil Responsibility, Protect Innocent People in Conflicts," United Nations 9042nd Meeting, SC/14904, May 25 2022, https://press.un.org/en/2022/sc14904.doc.htm.

22 "Reported casualties (cumulative) as of January 6 2026," United Nations Office for the Coordination of Humanitarian Affairs, using data provided by the Gaza Ministry of Health, https://www.ochaopt.org/content/reported-impact-snapshot-gaza-strip-6-january-2026.

23 Yehuda Teitelbaum, (@chalavyishmael), "Hamas' own data prove Israel is not 'indiscriminately bombing civilians'," sourced from Hamas Ministry of Health/CIA World Factbook, on Twitter (nowX),

August 12 2025, https://x.com/chalavyishmael/status/195530526
1154902514.

24 Thinkers such as John Selden, Richard Hooker, and Thomas
Coleman drew upon Hebrew scripture for Britain's new
constitutional monarchy. Eric Nelson, *The Hebrew Republic: Jewish
Sources and the Transformation of European Political Thought* (Harvard
University Press, 2011).

25 Melanie Phillips, *The Builder's Stone: How Jews and Christians built
the West—And Why Only They Can Save It,* (Wicked Son, 2025),
https://www.amazon.com/Builders-Stone-Christians-Built-West/dp/
B0DT15VDW6/ref=sr_1_1?

26 Liza Rosen (@LizaRosen0000), "Palestinian Muslims are freaking out
after this Australian TV host completely destroyed their false
narrative which always portrays Israel and Jews as the 'aggressors' and
the Muslim terrorists as 'victims,'" Twitter (now X), June 11, 2024,
https://x.com/LizaRosen0000/status/1755207068028453369?s=20

27 Palestine Liberation Organisation executive committee member
Zahir Muhsein in a 1977 interview with the Dutch newspaper
Trouw.

28 Barry Rubin and Judith Colp Rubin, "Who Is Yasir Arafat?" Foreign
Policy Research Institute, effective December 16, 2003, https://www.
fpri.org/article/2003/12/who-is-yasir-arafat/.

29 Auni Bey Abdul-Hadi, Syrian Arab leader to British Peel
Commission, 1937.

30 Myth: The Palestinians Have Never Had the Opportunity to
Establish Their Own State," The Centre for Israel and Jewish Affairs,
accessed January 12, 2026, https://www.cija.ca/palestinians_have_
never_had_the_opportunity_to_establish_their_own_state.

31 Noah Browning, "Abbas Wants 'Not a Single Israeli' in Future
Palestinian State," *Reuters*, July 29, 2013, https://www.reuters.com/
article/world/abbas-wants-not-a-single-israeli-in-future-
palestinian-state-idUSBRE96T009/.

32 Eyal Yakoby (@EYakoby), "Once Palestine is free, not a single
homosexual will be allowed to live in our pure land. Such perverted

abominations will not be accepted among us," Twitter (now X), https://x.com/EYakoby/status/1824141665109499939?s=20.

33   Eyal Yakoby (@EYakoby), "Fathi Hammad, senior Hamas official: 'All of you 7 million Palestinians abroad, enough of the warming up. You have Jews everywhere and we must attack every Jew on the globe by way of slaughter and killing,'" Twitter (now X), June 2, 2025, https://x.com/EYakoby/status/1929560999805300948?s=20.

34   "What Life Was Like in Britain During The Second World War," Imperial War Museums, accessed January 12, 2026, https://www.iwm.org.uk/history/what-life-was-like-in-britain-during-the-second-world-war.

35   Simon Parkin, "10 Facts About the Blitz and the Bombing of Germany," History Hit, September 5, 2021, https://www.historyhit.com/facts-about-the-blitz-and-the-bombing-of-germany/.

36   Jeffrey Herf, "Haj Amin al-Husseini, the Nazis and the Holocaust: The Origins, Nature and Aftereffects of Collaboration," Jerusalem Center for Security and Foreign Affairs, effective January 5, 2016, https://jcpa.org/article/haj-amin-al-husseini-the-nazis-and-the-holocaust-the-origins-nature-and-aftereffects-of-collaboration/.

37   Yona Admoni (Coblenz) and Moriah Michaeli, "False Flags and Real Agendas," Regavim, April 2025, https://www.regavim.org/wp-content/uploads/2025/06/RegavimSilufEng0406digital.pdf.

38   ILH Staff, "Pregnant Woman Murdered in Samaria Attack on Way to Give Birth," *Israel Hayom*, May 15, 2025, https://www.israelhayom.com/2025/05/15/pregnant-woman-murdered-in-samaria-attack-on-way-to-give-birth/.

39   "Number of Registered Live Births in Palestine* by Region and Governorate, 2007 – 2023," Palestinian Central Bureau of Statistics, effective October 16, 2024, link previously available at https://www.pcbs.gov.ps/statisticsIndicatorsTables.aspx?lang=en&table_id=3780.

40   "Humanitarian Access Improves Quality of Polio Vaccination Campaign in the Gaza Strip," World Health Organization, effective February 28, 2025, https://www.who.int/news/item/28-02-2025-humanitarian-access-improves-quality-of-polio-vaccination-campaign-in-the-gaza-strip.

41 Fahima Abbas, "In War as in Peace, Arab Israeli Physicians' Contribution to Israel Is Essential – Opinion," *The Jerusalem Post*, November 2, 2023, https://www.jpost.com/opinion/article-771253.

42 "Newest Medical Professor in Israel, Abdulla Watad, Just 35," American Friends of Sheba Medical Center, effective January 24, 2023, https://www.afsmc.org/2023/01/newest-medical-professor-in-israel-abdulla-watad-just-35/.

43 Abraham Bell and Eugene Kontorovich, "Palestine, Uti Possidetis Juris, and the Borders of Israel", *Arizona Law Review, vol. 58, pages 633-692 (2016), Northwestern Public Law Research Paper No. 16-04, San Diego Legal Studies Paper No. 16-214,* last revised October 7 2016, https://papers.ssrn.com/sol3/papers.cfm?abstract_id=2745094#.

44 Historical Section of the Foreign Office, "Syria and Palestine," *Peace Handbooks* 10, no. 60 (1920): 56, https://babel.hathitrust.org/cgi/pt?id=mdp.39015010785874&seq=398&q1=mixed+race.

45 James Parkes, *Whose Land? A History of the Peoples of Palestine* (Penguin Books, 1970), https://archive.org/details/whoselandhistory0000jame.

46 King Abdallah of Jordan, *My Memoirs Completed* (Longman, 1978).

47 "UN Says No Massacre in Jenin," BBC News, effective August 1, 2002, http://news.bbc.co.uk/2/hi/middle_east/2165272.stm.

48 "Lebanon PM Revises Air Raid Toll," BBC News, last modified August 7, 2006, http://news.bbc.co.uk/2/hi/middle_east/5252842.stm.

49 "The Diary of Ronald Reagan," Ronald Reagan Presidential Foundation & Institute, effective August 12, 1982, https://www.reaganfoundation.org/ronald-reagan/white-house-diaries/diary-entry-08121982.

50 William A. Orme Jr., "A Young Symbol of Mideast Violence," *The New York Times*, October 2, 2000, https://www.nytimes.com/2000/10/02/world/a-young-symbol-of-mideast-violence.html.

51 A poster of Al-Dura was seen in the video of Daniel Pearl's beheading. "Al-Dura: 'The Perfect Media Crime,'" *The Jewish Week*, September 28, 2007, https://www.nli.org.il/en/newspapers/jewishweekny/2007/09/28/01/article/37/.

52 Judea Pearl (@yudapearl), "I do remember Muhammad Al-Dura. His picture was projected behind my son, Daniel Pearl, in the last video taken of him, ostensibly to justify his murder," Twitter (now X), May 13, 2022, https://x.com/yudapearl/status/1525016542978506752?s=20.

53 I wrote about the al Durrah footage in "Faking a Killing" published in *Standpoint*, June 2008. The link is no longer available.

54 Anderson Cooper, "Deadliest Attack Yet in Gaza Crisis; Would-be Obama Senate Replacement Turned Away," *Anderson Cooper 360 Degrees*, CNN, aired January 6, 2009, https://transcripts.cnn.com/show/acd/date/2009-01-06/segment/01.

55 Matti Friedman, "An Insider's Guide to the Most Important Story on Earth," *Tablet*, August 26, 2014, https://www.tabletmag.com/sections/israel-middle-east/articles/israel-insider-guide.

56 Gordon Rayner, "Revealed: The Devastating Memo That Plunged the BBC into Crisis," *The Telegraph*, November 6, 2025, https://www.telegraph.co.uk/news/2025/11/06/read-devastating-internal-bbc-memo-in-full/.

57 John J. Mearsheimer and Stephen M. Walt, *The Israel Lobby and U.S. Foreign Policy* (Farrar, Straus and Giroux, 2008).

58 "Israel: Christian Numbers Rise, but Population Percentage Falls," OpenDoors, effective March 14, 2022, https://www.opendoors.org/en-US/research-reports/articles/stories/israel-christian-numbers-rise-but-population-percentage-falls/.

59 Jerusalem Post Staff, "Christian Population Declined 90% Under Palestinian Authority and Hamas – Study," *The Jerusalem Post*, December 23, 2024, https://www.jpost.com/diaspora/article-834585#google_vignette.

60 Lt.-Col. (res.) Maurice Hirsch, Tirza Shorr, "Demographics Don't Lie: The Decline of the Christian Population in PA- and Hamas-Controlled Areas," Jerusalem Center for Security and Foreign Affairs, December 22 2024, https://jcfa.org/article/demographics-dont-lie-the-christian-population-in-pa-and-hamas-controlled-areas-is-declining/.

61 Simon Rocker, "What the Koran Says About the Land of Israel," *The Jewish Chronicle*, March 19, 2009, https://www.thejc.com/judaism/what-the-koran-says-about-the-land-of-israel-qgkmcg33.

62 "Islam: Supreme Muslim Council Recognized Jewish Connection to Temple Mount," Jewish Virtual Library, accessed January 12, 2026, https://www.jewishvirtuallibrary.org/supreme-moslem-council-recognized-jewish-connection-to-temple-mount.

ACKNOWLEDGMENTS

• • • •

My grateful thanks to the many Jews in the communities I have visited whose personal accounts of what they have heard, witnessed, and felt since October 7, 2023, inspired me to write this book. May they all stay safe. I am particularly indebted to Dr. Ron Schleifer and David Olesker for their exceptional wisdom and insights about this issue. I deeply appreciate my splendid editor at Wicked Son, Adam Bellow, and my supportive agents, Neil Blair and Rory Scarfe at The Blair Partnership. And as ever, my husband, Joshua Rozenberg, continues to be the rock that shelters me and keeps my own head above the raging torrent.

ABOUT THE AUTHOR

Melanie Phillips is a British journalist, broadcaster, and author who has championed traditional values in the culture war for more than three decades.

She writes a weekly column for *The Times* of London and the *Jewish News Syndicate,* broadcasts on radio and TV, and gives public presentations across the English-speaking world. Her most recent book was *The Builder's Stone: How Jews and Christians Built the West and Why Only They Can Save It*, which was published by Wicked Son in January 2025. She blogs at melaniephillips.substack.com. For speaking inquiries, please contact info@1948talent.com.